After a Good Man Cheats: How to Rebuild Trust & Intimacy With Your Wife

CAROLINE MADDEN, PhD

TRAIN OF THOUGHT
PRESS

Publisher's Note

ISBN: 978-0-9907728-7-3

TOTP: AGMCP01262019

Summary: Guide for unfaithful husbands who want to restore trust & intimacy in their marriage.

Connie Johnston
Train of Thought Press
2275 Huntington Drive, #306
San Marino, CA 91108

www.TrainOfThoughtPress.com

TRAIN OF THOUGHT
PRESS

Dedication

I humbly dedicate this book to my clients who trusted me with their marriages and opened their hearts to me. I could never have written this book if I had not had the privilege of witnessing your journeys through what were most likely the most difficult experiences of your lives. Thank you for letting me in and allowing me to work alongside you as you labored to forge genuine intimacy in your relationship.

It is my hope that this book will help couples rebuild trust and intimacy. In this way, you (my clients, present and former) will also help those couples, as your collective wisdom and experience is delivered to those who currently struggle with the aftermath of infidelity.

CONTENTS

Introduction

You are a good man who made a bad decision. You were unfaithful.

You love your wife, and now that you see clearly what you have done, you are incredibly sorry that you have hurt her so much.

You want to save your relationship. You don't want to lose your family. If you could go back in time and stop the affair before it started, you would. In fact, you repeatedly kick yourself as you think back to the moment you knew you were crossing the line. You wish you could take it all back, but you can't.

Much as you desperately wish that she could just forgive and forget, your wife has made it clear that you can't just say you're sorry and expect everything to be as it once was. She feels the psychological impact of the affair, and this makes her angry... *very* angry. Her anger might even scare you at times. You've probably never seen this side of your wife before, and you hope you never will again.

Not only is your wife furious, but she's also emotionally volatile. Sometimes she seems to love you more deeply than ever, and other times she kicks you out of the house.

You are on a roller coaster. You want your marriage back, but you're not sure how to help your wife trust you again and move forward. She doesn't know what she wants, and her volatility exhausts and upsets you. You both are stuck.

My name is Dr. Caroline Madden. I've been a licensed marriage and family therapist in Los Angeles for almost two decades. I have helped countless couples restore their marriages after infidelity.

I've seen women *just like your wife* go through the whole process—from uncovering their husbands' affair to making it to the other side, heart healed and marriage restored. I have heard their innermost thoughts and concerns as they try to process their husbands' betrayal. I know what specific stages your wife will experience. I know what prevents women from moving forward, and I know what women need in order to trust and forgive.

Most importantly, I know the things men say and do that they *think* are helpful but that actually make things *worse*.

I also know what a difficult time this is for you. Your wife is hurting, but you are, too. I know that certain needs weren't met in your relationship, and I know you probably feel defensive and are sick of being the "bad guy." If you have children, you're probably terrified that you will be cut out of their lives and portrayed as the person who destroyed your family. You may wonder what was wrong with you that you felt the need to stray, or you may feel like she's blowing things out of proportion.

I know that you are doing your best to regain your wife's trust, but no matter what you do, you seem to make it worse.

That's why I've written this book. I want to hand you the tools to fix your marriage. I want to help you avoid the mistakes I've seen so many men make. I want to get you through to the other side as smoothly as possible.

This book will give you the power to anticipate her emotional needs and "get it" as you repair the rift in your relationship. She feels like life is a blur, but you can fix the problem by getting into her world, showing her you understand, and then helping her through the turmoil.

At a time when she is unsure if she can trust you, you can re-establish yourself as the good guy. The man who understands her. The person who loves her more than anyone else. The man in whom she believes and trusts.

This will help her truly believe that you are back for good.

This is the most important time for you to get things right, because your wife is actively deciding at this stage whether or not she wants to stay with you. Will the pain go away if she divorces you? Will staying with you just set her up for more pain?

This is a <u>proactive</u> book. It's a practical action plan that will walk you through the first stages after your wife has discovered the affair. You'll learn the things your wife will feel, say, and do, giving you the following:

- Insight into what she is thinking and why this is so hard for her
- Practical advice so you know exactly <u>what to do</u> at this important stage
- Actual scripts so you know <u>what to say</u> in response to specific situations
- <u>Clear explanations</u> as to why certain words and actions you think will be helpful might make things worse

Included at the appropriate points are <u>scripts</u> of what to say and why you need to say those words at that time. Do not just memorize these words and parrot them back to your wife. You have already lost her trust; if you start using words you don't normally use, you'll sound like you're faking it. You will want to translate the scripts into your own natural wording, using the meaning of each script as a launching pad for productive, healing dialogue with your wife.

Most couples who come into my office assume their marriage is over. They think infidelity is the worst possible thing that could ever happen, and they believe it means there is no hope. I've heard women say, "I can never trust him again," and in that moment, they believe it's true. I've watched many a grown man weep, thinking he may have lost all that he held most important in life.

And yet most of the couples that seek professional counseling after an affair survive the infidelity. As difficult as the process may be, many couples find the relationship is even stronger once they recommit and work through the experience.

I know you're not a horrible person (even though your wife probably says you are, and you may even believe that right now). You've made a series of bad decisions, but there *is* hope.
I can't promise you that your wife will take you back. However, I can give you the best chance and the best resources to make that possible. I'll also let you know why and when I think you should consider individual and/or couples counseling.

These tools are not a get-out-of-jail free card for multiple affairs. However, this book will help a sincerely repentant man who is committed to not cheating again. Right now you are saying and doing things that you think will help but are probably hurting your chances. This guide is meant to align your heart and good intentions with the most effective words and actions.

It is my hope that these resources will help you achieve your goal: to win back your wife and to restore your marriage so that it is stronger and more fulfilling than ever.

Chapter One:
Do You Really Want Her Back, or Are You Just Scared?

Before you even begin trying to repair your marriage, you need to evaluate: Do you really want your marriage back, or are you simply panicking and doing the things you think you are supposed to do? Before you do anything else, you need to figure out if you want to save your marriage. If you decide you do indeed want to save the relationship, you will need to determine whether or not you are willing to do everything that's required. Winning your wife back will be a marathon, not a sprint.

To figure this out, you will need to answer the following questions honestly.

Do you really want to save your marriage, or are you just scared?
There are good reasons to be scared of losing your wife. The following are just a few questions to consider:

• What are the financial implications of a divorce?
• How much will this hurt your children?
• What will your family think of you?
• Can you bear the loss of all that shared history?
• What if your Affair Partner (AP) is a poor life partner?
• What if you end up alone?

However, staying together because you are scared won't be enough. Fear is not a long-term motivator. It may help you do the right thing for a short while, but eventually you will be right back where you started.

Why do you think you cheated?
You went outside of the marriage for a reason. Now it's time to decide if you want to go through all the hard work of regaining

her trust and be 100% hers or if it's time to call it quits. Please take the quiz "**What Type of Affair Did I Have?**" at the back of the book to determine whether or not you had an *Exit Affair*.

I know you feel guilty. You probably feel like you are a bad person if you aren't willing to try to repair the relationship. But if you don't have your heart in it, it won't work. Also, you will probably just cheat again.

If you recommit, you will have to:

- Completely end the relationship with your AP
- Patiently work through all of your wife's pain and mistrust, which may take a while
- Prove yourself to be trustworthy, which may (at times) feel humiliating or like you are allowing her to control your life

Of course, there are benefits to recommitting. For example:

- You will reap the rewards of shared history, of years of experiences together, which is irreplaceable
- You will learn how to truly meet each other's needs
- You will bond on a deep level
- Your family will remain intact

To make this decision, take some time to think about the following:

- "What would my life be like 5, 10, and 15 years from now were I to stay? What if I leave?"
- "Why is my marriage worth saving?"

Is the Marriage Worth Saving? Why?
I know this may not be the "politically correct" thing to say, but sometimes a marriage isn't worth saving. While I never discourage a man from trying to save his marriage, I have listened to many men describe marriage dynamics that I know

are statistically likely to fail. In such cases, it may be better to focus on how to get out and move on.

What are your marriage dynamics? Right now is the perfect time for you to assess your relationship and to decide if your marriage is worth fighting for. You will want to consider the possibility that you engaged in an affair so she'd leave you or so there would be a reason to end the marriage. On the other hand, you might have engaged in an affair because you were unhappy with some aspects of your marriage but were not ready to leave. Perhaps the marriage is worth saving, which is why you didn't just divorce her and move on.

Now is the time to figure out if the relationship is a keeper or not.

Think back to when you first met your wife. Think of where you were. Think of how she looked. Then think of what made her "special." You know what I mean. I'm sure you dated a lot of girls before committing to your wife. Why her? What were those qualities that made her different from any other woman? Why did you fall in love with her?

Next, I want you to remember the day you proposed to your wife. How did you decide that you wanted to take that leap?

Close your eyes and spend some time thinking of that before going to the next section. I'll tell you why I asked you to do that later on in this chapter.

The Work of John Gottman

When evaluating whether a marriage is worth saving or not, I usually refer to the work of Dr. John Gottman. Gottman is a psychologist who is well known for his research regarding what makes couples work well together (and vice versa). His findings have been used to help couples improve relationship functioning and avoid behaviors that are harmful to relationships. In fact, he's spent the last 40 years making a name for himself in the counseling world for being able to predict, in a matter of minutes, whether a couple will remain married or get divorced based on the interaction styles that they show early on in their relationship. He does this (to a degree of 93% accuracy) through watching a short video of the couple discussing an issue of contention and looking for certain communication style traits. I like Gottman's work because it is based on facts and research and not just his personal theory.

Through years of research and working with over 3,000 couples, Gottman has determined that there are four communication styles that act as red flags in relationships. Gottman calls these the "Four Horsemen"—four behavior dynamics that have shown to predict which couples will divorce later in life and which couples will make it (Buehlman, Gottman, & Katz, 1992).

Gottman's Four Horsemen Are as Follows:

1. Criticism
Criticism means finding fault in your partner and assuming that the fault you identify is an underlying character trait, not simply a poor choice or weak moment. This includes *ad hominem* attacks that make your partner feel like he or she is fundamentally flawed and unlovable—not just that their behavior is *temporarily* annoying. Over time, criticism leads people to feel like they are unloved and unappreciated by their partner. I have found that this makes men, in particular, highly vulnerable to having affairs.

Example: Tom is late to dinner with his wife, Pam. Before Tom can even open his mouth, Pam says, "Typical selfish you. You can't even get to dinner on time. You don't care about me at all; you just care about yourself. I don't know why I even bother."

In this interaction, Pam leaves no room for understanding or forgiveness because she makes assumptions about Tom as a person, rather than focusing on the circumstances or his choices. Pam's disappointment is to be expected. However, if their communication style were healthy, she would express that she was upset with the fact that Tom was late while also letting him explain if he had (or did not have) a good reason for it. She would focus on his circumstances and choices, instead of making overarching assumptions and statements about his character. This would give Tom a chance to make amends, either by explaining why he was late or by apologizing for making a poor choice that made him late.

Criticism, as defined by Gottman, is dangerous when it goes beyond a complaint about an action or choice and becomes a label or assumption about a person's character in general. He terms it "negative trait attributions." Criticism destroys relationships because it taints how partners view each other on a fundamental level and erodes trust and emotional connection between partners.

2. Contempt

Contempt is when you treat your partner with disrespect and disdain as if he or she were "less than" you. There is an air of condescension. This type of behavior is exemplified by sarcasm, rolling of eyes, or words or actions that are meant to make your partner feel stupid, despised, and/or unworthy.

Example: Jesse discovered his wife Shelly eating out of the carton of ice cream right after she told him she was going on a diet. Jesse muttered, "Yeah right, on a diet," in a barely audible voice as he took the carton of ice cream out of her hands and put it into the freezer.

Instead of showing empathetic support and concern for Shelly, Jesse communicated with her in a way that likely made her feel hopeless and alone. His comments and actions suggested that he was disappointed in her and unable to understand her vulnerabilities.

Other examples of contempt include:

- Talking to your partner as if he or she is stupid or a child
- Mocking your partner instead of taking his or her feelings seriously
- Laughing or sneering at your partner
- Making biting jabs instead of talking sincerely and vulnerably
- Talking disrespectfully about your partner to friends or family as if he or she is not present
- Lecturing your partner

Contempt is extremely damaging to relationships because it communicates the message that one partner feels superior to the other or that the other partner is considered shameful, disgusting, or inadequate. Gottman considers this the most toxic of the Four Horsemen.

3. Defensiveness
Defensiveness includes responding to criticism (perceived or actual) with excuses or diffusion of blame instead of taking responsibility. Defensive communication blocks any perceived attack from a partner: "I might have hurt you, but you hurt me first." Defensiveness is often born out of pain and mistrust. It is based on the assumption that openness and vulnerability will only invite a partner to be critical and/or contemptuous in response.

Example: Tim came home from work to find the house is a mess. Tim felt distressed, but he didn't want to fight. Trying to seem like he wasn't too upset, he chuckled and lightheartedly asked, "Hey, what happened here? Did a tornado whip through the house?" His wife, Christine, snapped at him, saying, "Who are you to ask? You never pitch in!"

Christine showed defensive behavior by blaming the messy house on Tim. Examples of similar defensive responses include:

- "You think you always clean up while you're doing a project? Because you don't."
- "You think you could do better? Why don't you stay home with the kids once in a while?"

Defensiveness can destroy relationships because it circumvents open, intimate communication, and it is based on the unattainable belief that a person must be *perfect* to be loved and accepted. Healthy partnerships are instead based on trust that love exists for flawed-but-earnest human beings who believe in each other's good intentions.

4. Stonewalling

Stonewalling is when you withdraw completely refusing to interact with your partner, or when you give your partner the "silent treatment," giving no signs that you are tracking what your partner is saying. Stonewalling happens when you act as if your partner doesn't exist.

Example: Alex and Carla have argued about his daughter (Carla's stepdaughter) for years. Carla thinks he babies her; Alex thinks Carla looks for problems when they aren't really there. When Alex came home to find Carla raging about how his daughter snuck her cell phone into summer camp, he simply locked himself in the basement and started working on a project without talking with either of them first. After Alex retreated into the basement, Carla banged on the door, insisting he talk with her, but Alex responded by putting on his noise canceling headphones. When Carla texted him, saying they needed to talk, he turned off his phone. He refused to talk to her until she dropped the subject.

Stonewalling is a tactic I often see men use as a way to defend themselves after dealing with the other three horsemen (criticism, contempt, and defensiveness) for years. Men give up trying to communicate, and, in distress, shut down.

Using Gottman's Four Horsemen to Evaluate Your Marriage

As mentioned earlier in this chapter, Dr. Gottman found that couples who used these four negative communication styles when discussing difficult issues were more likely than other couples to divorce. By contrast, couples who stayed together over time tended to handle conflicts in ways that were more gentle, loving, and supportive.

Take some time to think about the ways that you and your wife communicate when you disagree or have differing expectations. If you recognize that these four toxic communication styles are typical for your marriage, you need to consider honestly if there are ways that you can replace such patterns. Because, unless you can replace the Four Horsemen with healthy, productive communication styles, there is a statistical probability that your marriage will end in divorce. Of course, these toxic communication patterns might have been what made your marriage vulnerable to an affair.

Is the spark still there, or is it all gone?

Remember how I asked you to think back to the beginning of your relationship?

When I asked you to think of first falling in love with your wife, did you have some sort of emotional reaction? Did you smile, or did you get sad? Were you able to list the things that made it worth committing the rest of your life to her?

If you had some strong, positive memories and felt a sense of longing and desire for what "once was," there may be something there to save. Maybe you had a solid foundation on which to build but your busy, stressful lives somehow got in the way and changed your dynamics. You may want to try to connect to those early positive memories and work towards rebuilding your relationship so you are both fulfilled.

On the other hand, when you thought back to the early days of your relationship, did you instead feel... nothing? Did you come up with thoughts like how she wasn't that beautiful, or did you remember things about her that annoyed you? Were you unable to access anything other than negative feelings towards her?

If you could only access negative feelings about her, that means (in my opinion) that the spark is gone. That was the best time in your relationship, the time when you felt closest to her. If you can't access those feelings anymore, then there may be no point in continuing your marriage. If your early memories of her are not at least somewhat glowing and happy, it's unlikely that you hold any romantic feelings about your wife. Certainly not enough to keep your marriage going.

I know, I know. There is a part of you that will always love her. But at this point it's probably more as a brother than as a lover, and your wife deserves to be loved fully. Romantically and otherwise. And the hard truth is, you will probably cheat again because your heart isn't in it anymore.

If you don't love her the way she deserves to be loved, it is selfish for you to continue in the relationship. Set her free so she can heal and find real love, with someone who respects and values her the way she deserves to be cherished.

What if you still aren't sure you are ready to recommit?
Before you try to repair your relationship, you must be willing to recommit to your marriage. If you are unsure whether or not you actually want to stay in your marriage (maybe you want to stay with your AP), please go to the end of the book (if you haven't already) and take the "What Type of Affair Did I Have?" quiz to see if the answer is "Exit Affair."

If you still don't know, then I highly recommend individual

therapy to determine what you really want.

Please don't begin the process of trying to rebuild trust with your wife if you're not sure you want to be in the relationship. You've already cheated on her and devastated her; please do not play games with her. Do not pretend that you're trying to work it out if you are still conflicted. That is selfish and cruel.

Additionally, if you think she is mad *now*, she will be *furious* if you continue to string her along and *then* break up with her. That will make for an ugly divorce. She stuffed her pride and tried to trust you again. She won't make that mistake again. She will feel the need for protection. She will lawyer up, and it will likely cost you more financially because... Well, "Hell hath no fury like a woman scorned!"

Chapter Summary: Determine if You Want to Save the Relationship

I know the pressure of the world is upon you to act repentant and promise to do everything in your power to win back your wife, but it's important that you first determine if this relationship is worth the time and effort required.

It's time to ask yourself the following questions:

"Is my marriage a keeper? Do I really think this relationship is worth saving?"

Answer: "No, I think it's time to throw in the towel."

Then that's what you need to do. Don't string her along. You might want to apologize for ending the relationship in such a hurtful way, but you will want to end things cleanly and quickly, with as much grace and respect as possible.

Answer: "Yes, my marriage is a keeper!"

Great! Then you are ready to proceed to the next chapter.

Chapter Two: How to Fix This Mess

So you have determined that you want your wife and marriage back. That's great; I'm truly happy for you. However, before you can help your wife, you have to do some internal work so you can get your head in the right space when you interact with her.

You might feel guilty, as if you are a terrible person. With this guilt may come many emotions that can interfere with the process of repairing the marriage. Two of the most common issues I hear men talk about in my office are the following:

- "This isn't fair."
- "I'm hurting, too."

It's important to deal with your feelings about these two issues before you try to fix your marriage.

1. This Isn't Fair

Paradoxically, coupled with the feelings of guilt, men also feel somewhat justified in cheating. They often say things like:

- "She wasn't meeting my needs."
- "Our marriage has been on the rocks for a while, and she didn't seem to care."
- "She didn't listen to me when I tried to tell her I needed more from her."
- "She had a part in this, too, but now I'm the bad one."

I believe you. It isn't fair. She probably wasn't meeting your needs in one way or another. You probably did try to tell her what you needed, and she:

- Didn't hear you,
- Didn't take you seriously, or
- Didn't respond.

However, *you* cheated. You went outside of the marriage instead of working it out. She had problems with you as well, but she didn't sleep with someone else. Even though she had her part in making the marriage vulnerable to an affair, it was your choice and your decision. You have to own up to this here at the beginning of the healing process.

I know how difficult it is to bite your tongue and take all the blame, but there is no other way around this.

I know she keeps asking you, "Why did you do this?" I also know it is tempting to tell her the harsh truth. You might want to say things like, "Because you never wanted sex," or "You were always busting my balls, and I felt I couldn't do anything right," or "I didn't even think you liked me anymore." But you must resist the urge to do this. At this stage of the game, saying these things will backfire on you. *Big time.*

Remember: She is still deciding whether or not she wants to be with you. Anything you say will sound like you are blaming her. She won't like that.

This is the bottom line: No matter what reason you give her, it won't stop all the why questions, because your reason will never be "good enough." Whatever reason you give, she will think to herself, "But that's not a good enough reason! It must be something else." Because to her, no reason is good enough! *It's a trap.*

Once you have regained her trust and rebuilt the intimacy in your marriage, *then* you can help her understand how to make the marriage less vulnerable to an affair. In fact, I strongly encourage you to do this, because you need to get your needs met so you aren't tempted to cheat again.

After she has made the decision to stay, she will want to know what made the relationship vulnerable to an affair. She won't want another affair to happen. However, *right now* she needs to know that it isn't her fault you strayed; she needs you to say it was your fault. This allows her to then shift from defending herself and proving she was a good enough wife to listening to why you think you cheated.

2. I'm Hurting, Too

If you fell in love with your Affair Partner, you may be experiencing a tremendous amount of loss. You may even feel like you are in an impossible situation. You love your wife, and you don't want to lose her, but you love your AP, too, and you can't imagine how you will live without her.

You may be feeling like:

- "My wife doesn't know how to meet all my needs, and I don't know if she ever can."
- "I'm giving up a relationship that has met so many of my needs, and that loss hurts."

Mourning after a breakup is normal. You may experience sadness and a recurring desire to reach out to your AP. You may also find yourself disconnected and lost in thought. You might not be able to sleep or eat due to your grief.

If your wife asks you what's going on, for God's sake, don't say, "I'm missing my [Affair Partner]." I'm hoping that is a no brainer. Unfortunately, more men than I can count have made this usually fatal blunder. The correct response is, "I feel like I don't even have a right to say this, but I feel so terrible and guilty. I feel like a bad person for hurting you."

It might be more difficult for you to get over your AP than you thought it would be. If you find this is the case for you, then maybe you should go into individual counseling to help you move through it.

I know this is a hard time for you and that you are in emotional pain. However, you cannot expect your wife to understand

17

(never mind sympathize with) your loss.

Your Decision: Preparing Yourself for the Challenge Ahead
After you work through your feelings about the injustice of being the "bad person" and your personal loss, you will need to evaluate the next step, which is to ask yourself the following question:

Are you willing to put your needs aside to save this marriage?
This is a big question. You may have determined that the marriage is worth saving, you might be ready to let go of your AP, and you may really want to make it work. That is fine and good, but you still have to decide if you have it in you to do the work required to repair the relationship. You will need to do the following:

*   Swallow your pride
*   Listen to her pain
*   Prove you are trustworthy
*   Open up to her
*   Lavish her with love

If you really want to repair this relationship, you will also need to:

*   Deal with your emotional "stuff" on your own for a while
*   Put her needs first
*   Focus on her 100%
*   Pull your weight (and extra) around the house and with the kids
*   Persevere until she can forgive and move on

This will take time. It will be painful. At times it will be exhausting.

However, you might get your wife back. She might even love you more than ever, and you might find ways to get your needs met inside your marriage in incredibly rewarding ways, if you do this right.

Chapter Summary: What's the Verdict? Are You Ready?
If you want to win her back, you will need to understand your wife is going through. I'll explain this to you in the next chapter. Do your best to enter her heart and understand what your infidelity has done to her. It's not going to be fun, but it will give you the tools you need to heal her.

By the way, I'm not trying to make you feel like a villain here. The fact is, if your wife doesn't feel that you "get" what she's going through, she won't be able to move on, so understanding her experience is important. This is the number one reason couples get "stuck" and end up in my therapy office.

Then we'll get into the practical part. Hang in here with me. In chapter six, you will find scripts that will save you when she comes at you with those angry questions. But you can't skip ahead to that until you understand what your wife is feeling. If you do, the scripts won't sound sincere, and therefore they won't work.

Let me explain to you why she's so upset. This insight will help you even when you hit a situation for which I didn't offer a script. The next chapter will help equip you as you communicate with her, diffuse her anger, and begin the healing process.

Chapter Three:
Understanding What Your Wife is Going Through
(AKA: Why is My Wife Acting Crazy?)

You need to know what your wife is going through so that you can gain genuine empathy. You need to grasp the enormity of what's happened and see how she views things.

Once you understand why your infidelity has hurt her, you can stay one step ahead of her. Like any negotiation, you need to know the "other side's" viewpoint. Knowing her mindset will help you understand why she is angry with you and what you can do (on the spot) to help her recover.

Understanding the Nuclear Bomb Phase
Your wife has just discovered your affair. I call this the *nuclear bomb phase* of affair recovery. Why? Because an emotional nuclear bomb has just gone off in your wife's life.

Right now your wife feels like the world that she knew has been annihilated. She feels like she is freefalling, unable to anticipate what to expect next. She doesn't know who you are anymore. The person she's trusted for years shared his life with someone else, and she didn't know it. Emotions, questions, doubts, pain—it's all flying past her as she grapples for something solid to hold. Something that won't hurt her, something that feels like safe, solid ground.

Your wife has experienced a significant degree of trauma. She feels especially shaken because the person to whom she normally turns when she is devastated (you) is the person who did this to her. She has been stabbed in the back, and the person who usually helps her handle pain in her life is the one who is twisting the knife.

Your wife probably feels:

- Helplessness
- Remorse
- Self-doubt
- Loss
- Depression
- Denial
- Anger
- Pain
- Guilt
- Fear
- Grief

Especially grief. Why? Because the marriage she thought she had is over. What she's got left—if the marriage even survives—will never be the same again, and she knows it.

In some cases, she may feel a sense of relief. She might have suspected that you've been having an affair for months if not years. Or she may have felt she couldn't "reach you" anymore. She might feel like she finally has the piece of the puzzle she needed to understand your distance or some of your other behaviors. Maybe she even mentioned that she thought you were having an affair, and you did more than just deny it—you called her "crazy." If you did this, be prepared for a lot of anger. You made her doubt herself and question her perception when she was right.

It's Like a Car Accident
Take a moment and think about your commute to work. Imagine that one day, on your way to work, a car suddenly crosses the median and crashes into you head on. Your car spins and flips over and over. You don't know what's up or what's down. Eventually things settle. They take you to the hospital, and you know that you are "safe" from the car accident.

Your broken bones heal. The insurance company replaces your car. But now you have to go back to work, on that same freeway. You'd be cautious, right? You used to trust that the other drivers on the road would follow the rules. Of course you had driven by more accident scenes than you can count. Accidents happen... to *other* people. Not *you*, because *you* are a safe driver.

But things have changed now. Whenever you hear brakes screech or other cars come a little too close to your car, you will instinctively panic, worried that you will be hit again. Right? Why? Because you now know that someone can upset your world in a second.

Over time, your fear will subside, assuming you don't have a second car accident. You'll be less shaky at the wheel.

This is how your wife feels. She's not even sure she wants to drive anymore, because she's not sure you're going to stay in your lane, and the last time you broke the rules, a devastating accident occurred. Viewing the affair and the trauma it has caused your wife as a bad car accident is an effective way for you to understand her experience. It will help you depersonalize her out-of-the-blue traumatic reactions (Rider, 2011).

Suddenly the Affair is Everywhere

Just like you wouldn't be able to help panicking after a car accident, your wife can't help but be triggered by affair reminders. In the beginning, this will be EVERY song on the radio. She will notice that TV shows and movies all have cheaters in them. (Where *strong* women *leave* their cheating husbands and *weak* women *stay* in their marriages.) If she caught you texting your lover, then you can bet that she will feel a trigger every time you text someone. She might not tell you, and she might not even make the connection between what you are doing and why she is suddenly so angry, but this will happen to her. Over and over and over.

This might feel like it's enough to drive you crazy, but it's important that you don't get upset with her. I know it's hard, but try not to personalize it. Think back to the analogy of the car accident. Imagine you just heard screeching brakes and started to panic.

When she gets upset, ask yourself: "What would I need to get over my panic?" Would you need someone to scream at you, "That was in the past. Get over it!"?

No. Of course not.

Now imagine the person who just said that to you was the guy who hit you and sent your car rolling. Think about how angry would you be. Just about as angry as your wife is when you say things like, "Why don't you trust me anymore?"

Post-Traumatic Affair Syndrome (PTAS)
I often talk with other therapists about relationships in general, learning from others who also work with couples. In these conversations, we sometimes use the term "Post-Traumatic Affair Syndrome" (PTAS) to describe the emotional experience a woman has after discovering her husband has been involved in an affair.

Why do we call it this? Because the symptoms women experience after discovering an affair are similar to the symptoms people experience after going to war or experiencing a significant trauma. They experience a form of Post-Traumatic Stress Disorder (PTSD).

Signs & Symptoms of PTSD
According to the Mayo Clinic, the following are typical symptoms of PTSD:

• Intrusive memories that make it difficult to function

- Flashbacks where the person actually feels like he or she is experiencing the trauma again
- Vivid dreams about the traumatic event
- Physical reactions (panic attacks, crying, shaking) as if the trauma or threat is still present

People who experience PTSD are shocked by how vivid the episodes are. They feel like they are back in the scene of the traumatic event, helpless to escape. Their bodies respond with an outpouring of adrenaline and a fight-or-flight response. Some people describe an episode as feeling like they are being held under water and must fight to get to the surface to get a breath of air.

Behaviors That Accompany PTSD
People who have PTSD often take certain actions to try to deal with the helplessness they feel. Some common behaviors are:

- Avoiding anything that reminds the person of the trauma
- Coping strategies such as oversleeping, overeating, drinking, substance use or abuse
- Excessive talking about the trauma as an attempt to overcome it

As a therapist, I often hear women lament that they cannot stop thinking about their husband's infidelity. They are frustrated with themselves. The thoughts upset them terribly, and they feel like they cannot control the recurring trauma.

These flashbacks and emotional responses often result in the following:

- Your wife's obsessive thoughts and urges to check in on you constantly
- Your wife's physical reaction of actually feeling panicked
- Your wife falling apart crying or venting her anger at you

- Your wife's flashbacks to the affair and the trauma of uncovering it
- Your wife feeling like she can't deal with this any longer, that the pain is too much

What She is REALLY Thinking...

If you could be a fly on the wall of my counseling office, you'd get to hear all the things women (like your wife) tell me they are feeling after they've discovered their husband's betrayal. I'm going to tell you some of the things women have told me. Chances are your wife is feeling most (if not all) of these things.

It's Not Fair!

Even though she wasn't perfectly happy in the relationship, she didn't cheat. Now she's in a position where she has to decide whether to divorce you or not.

Your wife probably feels like she is now between a rock and a hard place, forced to make a decision she never thought she'd have to make. It's important that you acknowledge that this isn't fair and that you give her the space she needs to make her decisions.

Maybe He Doesn't Really Love Me

Your wife is now confronting the infidelity "whys," mentally exploring the vulnerabilities of your relationship. She is constantly analyzing her memories, replaying instances that should have been clues, and wondering why she did not see that the marriage was in danger.

She is thinking about the external stresses on your marriage (work, kids, family, friends, travel, finances, etc.), but she is thinking even more so about ways she might have failed as a wife. Deep down, she is terrified that she is not good enough for you and that your infidelity is proof that you will never be happy with her.

She is probably thinking about every argument you've ever had. Weight gain, division of labor in your house, child rearing issues, work conflicts, lifestyle differences, how much sex you were or were not having... and she is worried that she may never be what you truly want.

This makes her feel both extremely vulnerable and protective of herself. You will need to assure her that she is everything you want and more and that you made a foolish choice you wholeheartedly regret.

It's Hopeless, So Why Even Try?

She will especially feel hopeless if you had discussed infidelity as a deal breaker. She is probably thinking: "You knew if you cheated, I would leave you. Therefore, you cheated as a way to exit the marriage."

Now you say you want to make it work, but she is struggling to believe you. She thinks you will try for a little while—out of guilt or just to look good—and then you will end the relationship.

You have to give her a reason to believe you are in this for good and that you somehow lost judgment even though you knew the terms and conditions.

Along those same lines, she is also probably thinking:

- "If you were so unhappy in the marriage that you did this, why would you ever want it back?"
- "We promised each other that if we were ever attracted to someone else, we would be honest with one another, but you didn't tell me!" (Yes, many couples have that agreement. I don't know one that has kept that promise.)

Your job is to help her recover hope that the relationship can work, because right now, she thinks it is doomed. Why should she try if it's just going to fail, and she will just get hurt more?

Who Did I Marry? Do I Even Want to Be With This Man?

The discovery that you have been unfaithful will undoubtedly shake her image of you. Women usually fall in love with men they trust and respect. She is now unsure of who you are and if you are someone she can trust and respect again.

She is thinking:

- "You've led a double life. Do I even know who you are?"
- "There are too many lies. How can I trust anything you say anymore?"
- "This was the one thing I *knew* for sure: that my man would *never* cheat."

This last point—this feeling that she thought she *knew* you, and she now realizes she didn't, is unsettling. This new knowledge results in a loss of innocence that she will have to mourn before she can even entertain the thought of trusting and loving you again.

You will need to support her as she mourns this loss of innocence in the relationship. You will need to assure her that you will let her know who you are and that you will do your best to be a man she can trust, respect, and love again. This will require repeated humility on your part.

I Need to Know the Truth

You may want to just confess and be done with it, but she will have what will feel (to you) like a million questions. Some of the ones that are certain to come up are:

- "Did you think of me while you were with her?"
- "Did you love her?"
- "Is she younger and/or prettier than me?"
- "When did it start? How? Why?"
- "How long did it go on? Where? When? How many times?"
- "What does this mean for us?"

She will need explanations from you regarding every one of these questions. You need to be prepared to calmly, gently, and respectfully answer every question she has, even if she repeatedly asks the same question. I'll provide scripts for each of these questions (and more) in chapter six.

Am I a Fool to Trust Him Again? Am I a Fool to Trust Myself Again?

She probably feels like a weak and stupid woman for staying. After all, popular TV, movies, and songs all tell her that only a foolish, weak woman with low self-esteem would stay with a man who has cheated on her. Her friends and family may also tell her (if she has opened up to them) that she is a fool if she stays with you.

It may help if you tell her that you respect her for even considering staying with you. Reinforce the mindset that strong women get all the facts and make decisions for themselves. Tell her you hope she will give you the opportunity to show her that she is right to trust you again.

Kool-Aid®, Not Just for Kids

In my practice, I use something I call the "Kool-Aid® analogy." Remember when you were growing up and your mom made Kool-Aid®? I don't even remember if it actually tasted like a specific flavor or if it was just called red Kool-Aid®, but you know what I mean.

When your mom opened the packet of Kool-Aid® and put it in the pitcher, it was fiery red. The more water she added, the lighter the red got. If she dumped a bunch of ice in, it would get lighter and lighter in color as the ice melted, right?

The packet of Kool-Aid® is the revelation of the affair. In the beginning, it will be fiery red.

Remember: Your wife is experiencing the psychological and accompanying physiological impacts not only of the affair itself, but also of the trauma of discovering the affair happened. She has PTAS. Because marital infidelity is a traumatic life experience that leaves a spouse profoundly wounded, her thoughts can become obsessive over the betrayal. Everywhere she goes, she sees things that remind her of the affair. These things act as PTAS triggers—that fiery red Kool-Aid®.

What is the water and ice? Time and trust. As you prove yourself to be a trustworthy man, over a period of time, the red Kool-Aid® will be diluted. She will stop seeing reminders. The reminders she does see will become less strong, less fiery red. Weaker in intensity. Easier for her to handle.

Unfortunately, the Kool-Aid® never completely goes away. I'm sorry, but even if you can't see the Kool-Aid®, it is still there. You will need to be prepared to deal with the ramifications of your infidelity for the remainder of your marriage.

Chapter Summary: Give Her What She Needs
The more you work to help her trust again, the more quickly the red Kool-Aid® will get diluted.

In a nutshell, your wife needs the following in order for her to forgive you and move on:

1. You repeatedly prove that you "get" her pain
2. You apologize
3. You promise not to do it again
4. You take responsibility
5. You change your behaviors

Your job is to help her believe that the pain will go away over time. You must convince her that you understand the gravity of your actions and how much you have hurt her as well as that you want to be the person who helps her heal.

In order to do that, you have some work to do. That work begins in chapter four.

Chapter Four: Get the Ball Rolling—
What You Need to Do RIGHT NOW

The first steps to healing your marriage entail dealing with the affair itself. You need to end the affair and promise yourself that you will never cheat again.

Let's get started.

Stop the Affair!
You have to end the affair.

Completely.

Entirely.

No "we'll just be friends" or "we'll tone it down."

You will need to say goodbye to your Affair Partner, making it 100% clear that you are done, that it is over, and that you will not come back. No leaving doors open.

If possible, do this in front of your wife. This way she will see that you don't have any secret conversations going on with your AP. No "if it doesn't work out with my wife, I'll contact you" kind of stuff. Your wife needs to see that you are serious about recommitting to her, and this is the only way to prove that to her.

Contact with your Affair Partner is more toxic to your marriage than a shot of heroin is to a heroin addict. Set yourself up for success.

I suggest that you call your AP in front of your wife and put the call on speaker phone. Your conversation should go like this:

"I'm calling you on speaker phone. My wife is on this call with me. I have decided to rededicate myself to my marriage. It's over. I will not be in contact with you anymore. I will not be contacting you to explain anything, and I will be ending all communications with you."

Don't give the AP any hope that there might be a chance to rekindle the relationship. Be clear, concise, and final.

I know that seems harsh. Something that I've seen work is calling the AP (from your office landline) and explaining to her that even though she was very special, your wife has found out, and now the affair is over. Then, let her know that you will be calling her later on speaker phone so that your wife will know it truly is over. This at least gives the AP a heads up on what you need to do so they aren't caught off guard or left thinking that you are a complete jerk.

Of course, you need to be prepared in case your AP doesn't want to cooperate. She is a person, too, and your AP may be angry that you are ending the affair. She may want to hurt you or hurt your wife because she doesn't want the affair to end, especially if you have led your AP to believe you might someday leave your wife for her.

It is possible that your AP may not be ready to end the affair and may try to keep things going. Or, she may want to "process" the ending of the relationship with you, wishing to believe she means more to you than "just an affair." Because of this, you should be prepared for your AP to try to contact you.

If your AP contacts you, reply with a short, simple: "I'm sorry if this hurts you, but I am rededicating myself to my marriage. That means absolutely no contact. I wish you well." Then hang up or hit send. If she writes or calls back, refuse to answer or delete her messages. Follow the script I will give you later to tell your wife about this contact with your AP.

Of course, this is complicated if you work with your AP (which is likely, since most affairs happen at work). If this is your situation, commit to always having a third party with you and the AP. Keep your emails that show this was a consensual relationship in case she goes to Human Resources to complain that you sexually harassed her. You might want to consider a new job or transfer to a different department if you either feel this will threaten your career or fear you will not be able to keep adequate distance from her.

Promise Yourself You Will Never Cheat Again

Now make a promise to yourself that you won't cheat again. Notice that I said to promise this to *yourself*. You need to get this straight in your heart and mind, independent of your wife.

Promise yourself this: If things get that bad again, you will divorce your wife instead of cheating again. View it as a decision regarding your character. You know that you are a good man. But even the best men make poor decisions. Good men don't make the same poor decision *twice*.

If you feel like the loss is difficult for you to handle, or if you are afraid that you will contact your AP again, set up an appointment with an individual counselor to work through your grief independent of your wife. Ask for help resisting the temptation to contact your AP, and again, make it an issue of character. Work to be the man you know you are capable of being: one of character, honesty, fidelity, and integrity.

To help yourself remain faithful, write out a list of reasons why you are making the choice to remain faithful to your wife. Include issues of character in this list. Keep it somewhere you can read it often. Make it your personal pledge of honor.

Chapter Summary: Man Up and Do What You've Got to Do

In summary, you need to immediately:

1. Stop the affair by contacting the AP
2. Promise yourself you'll never cheat again

After you have stopped the affair, you must win back your wife's trust by answering her many questions. Second only to stopping the affair, this is the most important point: You now must come clean with EVERYTHING, and once you have come clean, you must live in a completely transparent manner.

As a man, you have probably assumed she is angry because you had sex with someone else. That is only part of it. A smaller part than you may think!

She fears that she was a bad partner and that is why you had an affair. She doesn't feel like your "special girl" anymore because you were "special" with someone else. Her trust is broken. The best thing you can do is tell the truth.

However, there are *smart* ways to tell the truth and *stupid* ways to tell the truth. Helpful ways and hurtful ways.

The rest of this book will help you figure out how to come clean and handle all her questions without making a bigger mess out of things. Read on to learn how to do exactly that.

Chapter Five:
4 Steps to Handle Difficult Conversations

Like I said earlier: Telling the truth is essential, but there are smart ways to tell the truth and stupid ways to tell the truth.

You may have already said or done things that have exacerbated the problem. You may feel like you've blown it completely, or maybe you said she drove you to it, or that she deserved this because she didn't meet your needs.

Whatever has happened is now in the past. There's not much you can do about the things you've already said. Take a deep breath. If she hasn't called a divorce attorney and served you, there is still hope. (P.S. Even if she has, there is still hope.)

Be sure to pay close attention to the scripts provided. Review these scripts carefully, and tailor them to fit your communication style and situation. Remember, there are things that men think will *help* but that actually *hurt*. These scripts will connect with her. You'll notice the difference.

Step One: Help! She Wants to Talk!
Take it as a good sign if your wife wants to talk. At least she has agreed to be in the same room with you, and she isn't yelling at you.

When you do get a chance to talk to her, make sure you are:

- Loving
- Humble
- Gentle
- Remorseful
- Apologetic in tone
- Respectful of whatever response she gives you
- Willing to wait, but also willing to pursue her

She may need to be pursued, just to see that you care and you want to make things right. She might feel that if she brings things up you will get angry and defensive. When you aren't, and instead are willing to have a conversation, she will begin to really believe the affair is over. If you are so willing to talk about things, you aren't hiding anything currently going on.

Step Two: Apologize
Once you get her to speak with you, you must apologize and promise to never cheat again.

This sounds simple and obvious, but I have been surprised to discover that some men never do this.

You will have to apologize A LOT, so get used to this idea. This isn't just a one-time thing. But you need to start with one big, clear, heartfelt apology where you clearly and vulnerably say you are sorry and promise her that it will never happen again. How can she be expected to move forward if you don't commit to not hurting her in the future?

Don't be afraid to cry. I'm not saying manufacture crocodile tears, but if you have honest emotions, let them show. Show her that you are honestly and deeply remorseful.

Script:
"I'm truly sorry for the pain I have caused you. I hurt your feelings, and I feel like a piece of crap. I will never do anything close to cheating on you again."

Like I said, you will apologize multiple times. Make sure you do the following:

Accept the Blame
Hold yourself accountable for your decision to cheat instead of working things out with her inside the confines of the marriage. Use words like:

"It was my fault. Nothing you could have done made you deserve this."

Take Responsibility
Do not blame her or allow her to take even a small amount of the blame. Instead, say things like:

"I'm doing some deep soul searching, because clearly there is something wrong with me that I would have violated my vows to you."

Use the Proper Labels
Call it what it is—an affair. Don't mince words or try to sound more innocent than you are. If you refer to the relationship with your AP as a "friendship" or "slip up," your wife will feel like you are minimizing what happened. If you minimize the experience with your words, she will think you are also minimizing it in your heart, and she will not believe that you understand how serious this was for her.

If you don't take it as seriously as you should, you'll do it again because you didn't think it was that big of a deal. Why does this matter? Because if she can't trust you to remember, then she will have to remind you on a daily basis that it happened. (And not nicely, either.)

Don't Call It a Mistake
Don't ever call your affair a "mistake." It *wasn't* a mistake; you *purposefully* did this. There were several steps you had to take to be unfaithful and multiple lies surrounding your actions.

There are few words that will enrage your wife as much as calling your affair a "mistake" and/or an "accident." Using the word "mistake" indicates an unawareness of what you were doing. You made a decision. If you reject responsibility for your actions by always calling it a "mistake," she will have no way of knowing that it won't happen again.

She needs to be reassured that you know how badly your choices hurt her, you hold yourself responsible for those poor choices, and you will never hurt her this way again. Instead of calling it a mistake, use words like:

"I realize my actions hurt you. I betrayed your trust. I will never do it again."

Step Three: Promise *Her* That You Won't Cheat Again

You've already promised yourself; now you need to say it to her. Tell her how sorry you are that you hurt her. When you truly connect with her pain, it may at times be unbearable to you. Yet, you know that you need to understand fully how your actions affected her. You need to let her know that you realize that cheating was an unacceptable way to handle your problems and that from now on, you will deal with problems in the relationship head on instead of cheating.

Script:
"I promise you I will never, ever cheat on you again. If I am unhappy with something, I will talk to you and work things out with you, but I will not ever betray you again."

Step Four: Come Clean

Assure her you will tell her anything she wants to know. Then tell her everything. I will explain the reasons why you need to do this in the next chapter.

Script:
"Honey, there is no excuse for what I did. I am going to tell you the whole truth. As painful as it is to hear, it is embarrassing to tell. I'm scared that if I tell you the whole truth, you will definitely leave me. But if I am even going to begin to build trust with you, I know I need to tell you the truth."

Then DO IT! Tell her the truth. I know it's scary. I know that you have already tried to talk to her and explain things, and it has gone terribly wrong. That's why I have provided scripts for the most commonly asked questions and situations in the next chapter.

Chapter Summary: Take Those Steps

Telling the truth the smart way is essential to repairing your relationship. You will face some tough questions, but reviewing these scripts will help you come up with truthful answers the *right* way. Each of these four steps will help you approach those difficult conversations and not make things worse.

Chapter Six:
Answer Her Questions
(AKA: What to Say!)

No doubt she has asked you a million questions, and chances are she will ask you many more. You probably feel like you are standing in front of a batting machine, getting pelted with curve balls before you can even position your bat.

Why is she asking all of these questions? And why should you answer every single question she asks?

Because:

1. She wants to understand the reality she was actually living in.
2. You have all the information. That creates a power imbalance and leaves her feeling extremely vulnerable.
3. Trust me when I say that she already knows more about what you did than she lets on. She is checking to see if you are still lying. She can't begin to trust you until you stop lying and protecting yourself.

The NSA, FBI, and CIA are amateurs compared to a wife who has been betrayed. At some point she will check all phone and credit card statements. She will look through all your emails (including work ones) and private Facebook messages. Some women have found a way to download all text messages.

No matter how sick you are of answering the same questions over and over, you can't say, "I'm done talking; no more questions." Let me explain why.

Why It's So Important to Come Clean
Women repeatedly tell me that what made them leave the relationship WASN'T the AFFAIR! It was the drip, drip, drip of the truth that slowly leaked out over a long period of time.

They would just get used to the facts that had been revealed thus far, and they would just start to adjust and try to trust and move forward, and then BANG! More information would surface.

Why is this so damaging to the relationship? It makes women feel like they will never get the whole story and can never fully trust that their husband is being completely honest.

You may think that the drip, drip, drip method is kindest. You don't want to overwhelm her with all the details of what happened. You're afraid that if you tell her the whole truth, she will leave. But how can she move on if you are still lying? Omitting information that she needs to make her decision as to whether or not to stay with you is a yet another form of lying.

It's best to rip off the Band-Aid® all at once so she knows everything that happened and can decide with eyes wide open if she can indeed forgive you or not. She deserves to know the truth. You owe her this much.

How to Tell the Truth
While I've told you to tell the entire truth, that does not mean you need to torture her with details. Some details are important to share, and some details should never be disclosed.

For example, DO NOT tell X-rated details. You should expect her to ask for details, but you can't give in, even if she claims she can handle it.

If you tell her X-rated details, those details will haunt your relationship forever. Even if she decides to stay with you, she will never forget them. Long after she has forgiven you and moved on, she will still think of how you made love to another woman, and the specifics you gave will sabotage your physical relationship because she may not be able to forget them.

Script:

"I agree with you that you have the right to all details regarding what I did. I worry that if I go into detail about the sexual relationship, it will hurt you more than I have already. If, in a month, you still want to know the details, I will of course tell you at that time."

In a month, she will be happy that you didn't tell her. She will think to herself, "I'm glad I don't know the details." She just needs to get out of this nuclear bomb phase before she will know what she needs to best protect herself.

The nuclear bomb phase is crazy-making. At this point, she wants all the information because she is so angry about being deceived, and she isn't capable of evaluating what is good and what is bad for her.

In a month, you will have truthfully answered her most important questions and will have shown through your actions that you are remorseful. You need to tell her how you hid things from her, but she doesn't need sexual details.

If, in a month, she still wants to know the sexual details, then you will have to tell her. Be factual and not salacious.

What to Tell

Do tell:

- How it started
- If it was physical
- If you used protection
- If it was more than once

The following are typical questions and topics most women want to discuss after an affair. Pay attention to the scripts and be sure always to tell the truth—the smart way!

Q: "How did it get started?"

Tell her the basics of how you got involved. When you first met, when you realized you were more than friends, when you crossed the line. DO NOT romanticize or minimize what happened. Tell the facts. Do not give details that might hurt her, like how sexy your AP looked or how you started fantasizing about her. Tell the truth of what happened but do not hurt your wife with details that might destroy her self-esteem.

Example: You met your AP (let's call her Jennifer) at work. You slept with her when you said you were working late. It's been going on for three months.

Script:
"I met Jennifer at work. We were assigned to a project together. I was excited about the great work we did on the project. We spent a lot of time together alone and got too close. It got physical one night when we were working late. It happened five times. Once at the office and four times at her place. We used protection every time. I have already ended it, but I can call her and tell her it's over again with you here listening in on the call if that will help."

Q: "How long did it go on?"

You will need to be honest, even if you fear this will be a deal breaker. If you say it only happened once and she finds out it happened for two years, you are headed for divorce court.

Example: You've been having an affair with an old girlfriend, Susie, online for the past year, and you met up with her in person twice.

Script:
"I've been emailing with Susie almost daily for the past year. At first I thought we were just catching up, but then we became

more than friends, and it turned into an affair. I should have shared everything with you, and I chose to share with her instead. You are the one who knows me best. I should have trusted you with this information.

"I used to email her after you went to bed, on those nights I stayed up later than you. I lied and said I was working.

"We slept together twice, on business trips that took me to her city. She lives in Chicago.

"I realize that this hurt our relationship and belittled what we share. I am so sorry I let it go on this long."

Q: "Why did you cheat?"

Your wife will ask you over and over again all kinds of "why?" questions. With certain questions, it won't matter how you answer; she will be pissed at you no matter what you say. She is trying to find "the answer"—that perfect answer that finally helps her understand why you did what you did.

But here is the rub: There is no right answer because there is nothing that you can say that will justify in her mind why you had an affair. *Therapy will figure this out*

So what are you supposed to do?

You will just have to suck it up and show her how sorry you are!

Script:
"There is nothing I could say that would answer this question without it sounding like a list of excuses to justify my affair. I am doing some deep soul searching right now. I have to figure out why I did this. As I explore these things within myself, I hope to share this knowledge with you."

Q: "Did you love her?"

The best situation is that you didn't love your AP. You need to be honest with your answer, but you need to be careful not to hurt her unnecessarily. You especially need to be honest if there are emails, texts, etc. in which you said, "I love you." Even if you have deleted them, your AP might not have. Therefore, it is possible that your wife will find out.

It is best that you say you never loved her. You slept with her for the thrill.

Script:
"I never loved her. Not one bit. It was a purely physical experience. I was selfish and made a stupid choice to indulge in a sexual desire that I now see has hurt you so much. It happened X number of times. To think that I have done this to you for a selfish decision made in lust is soul-crushing for me, and I just can't believe how stupid it was.

"It was a stupid, selfish choice, and I wish I'd never done any of it."

Let's say you were in love with her. Perhaps your wife has discovered emails, texts, etc. where you said that you loved your AP.

Script:
"I thought I was in love with her for a while, but I see now it was just lust. I was caught up in fantasy. I see how insignificant my relationship with her was in comparison to what we have in our marriage. You know me. What we have is real. I was like a stupid schoolboy.

"You mean everything to me. You are the woman I love, and she is nothing compared to you. I did not see things clearly for a while, but now I know I only want to be with you for the rest of my life."

If you want to save your marriage, do not say, "Yes, I love her and I am sad that we can't be together anymore." Those are feelings you will have to work through on your own, independently.

Q: "Did you think of me when you were with her?"

If you did think of her, you should say the following:

Script:
"I'm ashamed to say that I did think of you. I fooled myself into believing that if you never found out, it wouldn't hurt you. That was wrong. Spending time and energy with another woman would hurt our relationship even if you never found out."

If you didn't think of her, you should say the following:

Script:
"I didn't. On a deep level I must have understood that what I was doing was wrong, so I must have just compartmentalized my AP from my real life."

Q: Is she younger and/or prettier than me?

Oh, boy. Your wife is terrified that you cheated because she is not good enough for you. She fears that she is not pretty enough or young enough and that you will no longer value her as she ages. It is essential that you get this right.

If the answer is yes, she is younger than your wife, you should say the following.

Script:
"She is X years old. Just saying that makes me feel like a jerk. I'm so ashamed that I was 'that guy' who cheated on his wife with someone younger.

"I can't believe that I was willing to risk everything just to pump up my ego. It was stupid and selfish."

However, if your AP was the same age/beauty level or not even as pretty, then your wife will really think it was about you not liking your wife anymore. It will feel more personal to her. This might not make sense, but it is easier for a woman to deal with her husband sleeping with a young, hot girl. She will chalk it up to the idea that "all men are dogs" but not take it as personally.

If your AP was the same age and not much prettier than her, you should say the following.

Script:
"She is X years old. I think that had she been some hot 23-year-old, I would have seen what was happening and immediately avoided her. Because she was my age, I see now that I didn't protect our marriage the way that I should have. It was a slippery slope I fell down."

If she is prettier, you will need to think this through.

Unless your AP is objectively a couple of points higher on the beauty scale, then say no.

If everyone would think your AP is prettier than your wife:

Script:
"It isn't about her looks. If a naked supermodel seduced me, my answer should be, 'No, I'm a married man,' and I should walk away. I blame no one but myself."

Q: "If you knew I would leave over infidelity, why did you still choose to cheat on me?"

Script:
"I honestly didn't think it through. I don't want to leave you; none of this was ever to leave you."

Q: "Was it better with her? Are you unhappy with our sex life?"

It's important that you make her feel special and like she is number one, even if the sex was better or wilder with your AP. You will lose your wife if she thinks she is number two.

Example: It wasn't better.

Script:
"It wasn't even close to what we share. I knew right away that it was the stupidest thing I've ever done. I'm so sorry."

Example: It was better, but you only slept with her once.

Script:
"It wasn't even close to what we share. We are in love, and when we have sex, it's making love. What happened with [AP] was just physical, just sex. I never should have done it, and I will never do it again."

Example: It was better, and you slept with her for a long period of time. In fact, your sexual relationship with your wife has been nonexistent or disappointing for a long time now, and you wish you could have the sexual relationship you had with your AP—but with your wife.

Not surprisingly, this may be the most common reason I have found that good men cheat. Nine tenths of the relationship is pretty great, but the one tenth of the relationship that is bad is the sexual aspect.

You've tried everything, yet she still doesn't seem to be into sex with you. Or, if she does have sex, it is what I call "tick tock" sex. As in go ahead, have sex, but don't take too long. I know that is soul-crushing, and I'm so sorry you have had to be in that position for so long.

This is critical and will have to be addressed. It just can't be addressed right *now* because it will sound like you blame her for the affair.

However, most of my female clients state up front that their husbands wanted sex and they repeatedly turned them down. It's in a woman's nature to blame herself for everything. Even though she isn't saying it, if you cheated because she made the relationship vulnerable by not having mutually connected sex with you, she has probably begun "getting it," even without you saying a word.

If she doesn't get it, then you will have to get into marriage therapy.

In any case, right now you need to apologize and give her time to deal with the fact that you cheated on her. Hopefully you will get this part of the relationship worked out after you win her back.

Script:
"It wasn't even close to what we share. I do miss the way things were between us in the beginning, when we used to make love a lot. I thought what I was missing was sex, but what I was missing was making love to you and connecting with you. I'm hoping we can find ways to get close like that again."

Q: "Has she contacted you?"

Your wife is terrified that this isn't the end of the trauma, but rather, that this will to continue for weeks, months, even years. She is not sure she can handle the pain she has already experienced, never mind the tremendous pain she would feel if you continue the relationship.

You need to answer this question honestly, because in many ways, this is even more important than what happened before she found out about the affair.

Example: Your AP has not tried to contact you.

Script:
"No, she has not. I have made it clear to her that I am rededicating myself to our marriage and that we are not to be in contact in any way. If she does contact me, I will let you know and ask how you want us to respond."

Example: Your AP has managed to contact you. Let's say she showed up at your place of employment and waited by your car for you after work one day.

Script:
"Yes, she waited for me outside of work, in the parking lot, but I told her I had nothing to say to her. I told her that I am rededicating myself to our marriage and that we are not to be in contact in any way. If she contacts me in the future I will let you know ASAP, and we will decide together as a couple how to respond."

Example: You work with her and see her every day.

Man, this is hard. Every wife is different. Some will want to hear the details of every interaction you have with your AP, while others will want to tune it out. You need to ask your wife what she needs to feel safe. Be open to your wife wanting you to get a new job.

My advice is to always have a third person present. Try not to work late. If you have to work late, give your wife plenty of advance notice and invite her to come by the office anytime.

What if your wife wants to call the company, HR, the boss, etc.? Yes, wives have done this.

Script:
"Of course you are angry. I know I should have thought of the consequences of all of this, but obviously I didn't. If you call my

work, I might get fired, and that will affect all of us. She might lie to defend herself and say it wasn't consensual. [Which, by the way, is a definite possibility.] Me losing my job isn't going to help our situation."

What if You Are Too Scared to Tell the Truth?

You may find yourself too afraid to answer some of her questions. If that happens, use this script to explain how you feel.

Script:
"I know that I promised to answer all your questions, but that question is a bit overwhelming. I'm scared. I promised that I would never lie to you again. Please give me some time to summon up the courage to tell you."

Don't take forever. Then approach her, saying, "I'm ready to answer the question."

Do not wait so long that she ends up approaching you again. That will make her feel needy and powerless. That leads to anger and control issues. Trust me: It will be worse for you if you delay too long!

Prepare Yourself to Answer These Questions More Than Once

You may be tempted to get impatient with your wife when she asks you (for the 15th time) why you cheated on her. However, you need to answer her questions patiently and with as much sincerity as the first time she asked you.

Why does she ask you the same questions over and over?

1. She is trying to trap you in a lie and find out if there is more to the story.

2. She is thinking of all the times she thought you were happy when you were actually sleeping with someone else. This will

happen especially when she looks at pictures. She will think, "I thought we were so happy." Every time she thinks this, she will mourn the loss of trust and innocence in your relationship.

3. She is trying to figure out how she was fooled. In short, she is trying to wrap her head around the reality she has been living in so that she will be prepared (in the future) to recognize the signs if you are cheating on her again. She is asking the questions as a way to protect herself from ever feeling this degree of pain in the future. She is thinking that if she understands how it happened, she will see it coming (if you cheat again) and will not be hit out of the blue again.

Expect Her to Get Angry and Cry a Lot
When your wife gets overly emotional, feels the need to tell you about some little thing that reminded her of the affair, or says she doesn't know if she can trust you again, you need to remember that she is experiencing PTAS.

Remember the car accident analogy. Ask yourself what you would need when you began driving again after a life-threatening accident, especially when some idiot swerved in front of your vehicle, barely missing you.

You would need to lean on someone as you calm yourself. Your wife needs you to comfort her and assure her that you understand why she is so upset.

Script:
"It's understandable that you feel this way. I did something that devastated your trust. I am here and will do everything you need me to do so that you feel safe again."

If she is like most women, she has told herself and others that if a man ever cheated on her she would be "so out of there." Now she is looking around and realizing that it just isn't that easy. The world isn't black and white. Maybe you share a house and kids. She enjoys her position in society as a married woman.

She dreads the thought of going into the singles scene at her age. Let's not even start with the idea of being a single mother! It's important that you are patient with her, even if she gets so angry that she screams or has to leave for a while. Remind yourself that you have hurt her tremendously and that people can be highly volatile after being traumatized. The only way to win her back is to be patient and comforting and to show her that you still love her, even if she gets upset over and over again.

Take advantage of the fact that she still hopes this is all just a bad dream and she will wake from it. She is programmed to love you, trust you, and be comforted by you. You created this hole in her and ironically, you are the only one who can heal her. She will fight this for a long time, but eventually she will come to understand that she needs to move through this. Give her every reason to believe that you love her and realize that you did a bad thing which you will never do again.

Ten Things You Should Never Say

I've walked you through some specific scenarios, but will probably encounter questions I haven't covered. The following are good rules of thumb to memorize before you start talking about the affair. These are ten things you should **never** say to your wife:

1. "It was a mistake."
2. "It was an accident."
3. "I didn't tell you because I didn't want to worry you."
4. "Can't we just move on from this?"
5. "Are you STILL angry?"
6. "Why did you check my phone/email/Facebook?"
7. "It didn't mean anything."
8. "Yes, the sex was better. "
9. "I'm not sorry I did it."

Most importantly, ***do not ever*** say:

    10. "Don't blame her. She is a good person."

Meaning your Affair Partner. Don't do *anything* that seems like you are defending your AP. Part of what is destroying your wife is she realizes that you aren't on the same team anymore. You were on a team with someone else. Anything that seems to align you with your AP will be met with extreme anger.

P.S. There is nothing you can say that will ever convince your wife that your Affair Partner is a "good person." Nothing. In her mind, "good people" don't sleep with other women's husbands. And no, it doesn't matter whether or not your Affair Partner knew you were married.

Chapter Summary: Coming Clean

Coming clean is never easy. Expect your wife to need some time to process this after you answer all her questions. She may need time to be alone or to go stay with her sister or a friend for a while. She may want you to hold her while she cries. She may storm out, or she may ask you to go away.

Honor her requests as best you can. Be patient. I know this is the scary part, but honesty really is the best policy. If you get all the awful truth out in the open, she can make the decision that is right for her. It will speed up the process of deciding if she can stay with you or not, and, if she decides she *can* stay with you, it will speed up the healing of the relationship.

In chapter seven, you'll learn what to do to start rebuilding trust and intimacy with your wife. If you make it through the coming clean phase and then invest in the rebuilding phase, you've got a good chance at making the relationship work.

Here is the good news: you have a good chance of fixing this mess if...

1. You come clean in one fell swoop and don't drip, drip, drip the information out to her.
2. You apologize repeatedly and promise not to do it again.

If, after the first couple of months, she hasn't served you with divorce papers, she is leaning towards staying. If you give her every reason to believe that she isn't a fool for doing so, she may realize that she will be married to a grateful husband who knows she was strong enough to leave but didn't.

The next challenge is to make sure you foster a marriage with someone who isn't bitter and angry and bringing up the affair in every fight for the next 20 years.

Chapter Seven: Carry the Ball

You've 'fessed up. You've come clean. You've made promises.

Now it's time to show your sincerity through your *actions*.

It's not enough to have caught the pass. You now have to carry the ball down the field and prove that you will never fumble again. If you don't show your wife that you "get it" by changing your behavior, there's no way you can expect her to move forward.

There's more to this plan than just saying you're sorry. You now know how much you've hurt your wife, and you've done your best to apologize and help her understand that you still love her and want to be with her. But now you need to start healing her so she can invest in making the relationship better.

It will be easier for you to put the past behind you because you know what's in your heart. You know that you're willing to commit to the marriage. You know that you said goodbye to your AP. You want to forget the affair even happened and just focus on rebuilding the relationship so it's stronger and better than it's ever been.

However, your wife has no way of knowing this. She *used* to trust you, but you abused that trust and betrayed her.

That means she feels like she has to stay on high alert in case you don't "get it" and won't keep her safe from pain. She is watching everything you do to see if she can trust you, trying to determine whether or not you really "get it."

Actions Speak Louder Than Words
You've said the right words; now you need to prove that you mean what you say through your actions.

You will need to:

- Initiate working on the marriage to rebuild trust
- Seek therapy, talk with your minister, or seek help from a group
- Change your behavior in significant ways
- Save her from further pain
- Apologize repeatedly
- Demonstrate that you can be trusted

This chapter explains the practical steps you should take to prove (through your actions) that you are sincere and genuine in your recommitment to your marriage.

Initiate Working on the Marriage

You may think it's obvious that you want to improve the marriage, but this is not obvious to your wife. You need to make it clear to her that your marriage is your number one priority right now. To do this, you need to do the following:

- Verbalize your intent. Tell her that you are prioritizing the marriage in every way you know. Ask her what she would like to see you do to make the marriage better.
- Pay attention to what she says she needs. When she tells you something that she thinks would make the marriage better, write it down and then make sure you actually do it. For example, if she says it would help her feel better if you were home from work every day by 6:00 p.m., make sure you are home every single night at 5:55 p.m. If something happens and you are going to be late, call and apologize.
- Make time for just the two of you. Get a babysitter (and when I say this, I mean *you* should book the sitter, not ask her to do it) and take her out someplace special. Make a habit of spending time together, just the two of you.
- Don't act like business is as usual. She doesn't trust you. Every time you leave the house, she wonders where you are really going. She looks around the house and thinks to

herself, "Maybe I can handle being single; he's gone so much anyway." In the first couple of months, you need to stay close to home! Are you usually out with the guys on Wednesday nights to play basketball? Drop the team for a while and spend all your free time with your wife or the kids or doing things to support her.

Tell her that you consider the marriage more important than anything else. Your initiative will show her that you care. She needs proof of that right now; you will need to make your intentions loud and clear so she can start to trust you again.

Start Therapy

For most men, going to therapy is a big gesture. Your wife probably knows this. As a result, this will go a long way with your wife because it will help her to believe that you are taking the marriage seriously.

The following are reasons to go to individual therapy:

1. To grieve the loss of your AP in private, in a way that will not hurt your wife
2. To appease your wife (if she asks you to go)
3. To deal with all the anger that your wife is directing towards you
4. To discover the internal/family of origin reasons that might help you understand why you cheated
5. To get help if you think you might be a sex addict (use the quiz at the back of this book as a starting point)

Therapy is not only helpful in its own right, but it is also a card you can pull out at any time.

"I'm working hard in therapy trying to figure out how I could have done this."

"I'm in therapy; clearly I need to be fixed."

"My therapist is helping me to explore things in my childhood that could have led me to feel this was okay."

"You've brought up some great points in this conversation. Would you mind if I reviewed them with my therapist?"

In other words, going to individual therapy will not only help you personally, but it will also help your marriage.

But shouldn't we be in couples counseling?
This might surprise you, but I think too often couples rush into therapy. It takes a highly skilled therapist to stop the hemorrhaging while exploring what made the relationship vulnerable to an affair. If it is too soon, the wife will feel like both her husband and the therapist blame her for the affair. As mentioned before, a woman is usually in a nuclear bomb phase at first and doesn't comprehend information too well. Also, some therapists rush physical intimacy before the wife is ready. The wife feels forced, and that produces negative feelings in both partners.

It would be better for you to seek individual therapy, establishing that you are the one who did something wrong. After a month or so, state that your individual therapist believes that couples counseling would be helpful.

Please see a pro-marriage therapist. If possible, see one that specializes in affair recovery. At the very least, see a Licensed Marriage & Family Therapist. An MFT is trained in relationship dynamics and will see the affair as part of an overall system and not just that you are an awful person.

Go to Church
Of course, if you're not religious, I'm not saying you should "find Jesus" or that religion is essential for your marriage to recover. However, if you and your wife have been religious in the past, going to church now will help your wife trust that you

are repentant.

Going to church will help because:

- Most churches are family-based and pro-marriage
- Your wife will be supported in her desire to keep the marriage together—forgiveness is viewed as a virtue
- If your wife sees your infidelity as an issue of morality, she will see that you are making efforts to get back on track

Meet Privately With a Minister/Counselor

If you initiate a meeting with your minister or a counselor, seeking guidance, your wife will see that you are proactive in getting help with the marriage. You can initiate with a secular counselor or with a counselor from your church, whomever you feel would be most assuring to your wife.

If you are Catholic, I recommend that you meet with a lay minister and not the priest. You need to work with someone who is actually married and understands how hard it is. (I say this as a person who was raised Catholic.) Also, these days the priest's time is spread pretty thin. If your wife wants you to seek moral guidance, sooner is better than later.

Talk to your wife and see if there is a man that you both agree is a good example of a faithful husband. Confess to him and ask for help. She will see your willingness to be vulnerable with another man as a significant sign of genuine remorse.

Ditch Any Bad Influences

If she knows that you have friends who were aware of the affair (and did nothing to convince you to stop), or worse, enabled the affair by providing alibis, stop being friends with them. Tell your wife that you now recognize that "you are the company you keep." Tell her you now realize that a good friend would have told you to stop and to rededicate yourself to the marriage. These friends didn't support your marriage, so you are distancing yourself from them.

Help Your Wife Take Care of Herself Physically, Mentally, and Emotionally

Your wife will most likely get angry with you and/or break down crying frequently in the early months. Your response always needs to be one of compassion.

When She Cries

You will find her crying over the betrayal. More than once—in fact, it may be a frequent occurrence for a while. You may feel like she has cried enough already or like she is trying to rub it in or punish you. Although this may be true, there are multiple reasons for her tears:

- She really is devastated and doesn't know how to process that devastation
- She fears she is not good enough for you, and that fear also may have spread so that she now wonders if she is good enough for anyone—you may have damaged her self-worth as an appealing woman
- She needs you to see how much you hurt her, and she is afraid you don't get it
- She is indeed trying to punish you, and she needs you to accept the punishment in order for her to forgive you

When you find her crying, you need to open yourself up to her instead of making her feel ashamed or embarrassed for crying. You need to affirm her, letting her know that you recognize her right to mourn. You also need to comfort her and assure her you will not hurt her like this ever again.

Script:
"Of course you're feeling sad. What I did was awful and hurt you tremendously. I can't take that away, but I want you to know that I will spend the rest of my life recommitting myself to this relationship and proving that you are not a fool for trusting me again."

When She Blows Up at You

There will be times when your wife will get extremely angry. She might yell, scream, throw things, threaten to move out (or throw you out), or even leave for a while, saying she doesn't know if she can ever forgive you.

Don't be surprised by this, even if she was loving and initiated sex the previous day. Remember, little things trigger her PTAS all the time. Perhaps last night she felt hopeful, like she might forgive you. She was grateful that you were making it through this harrowing experience, so she put forth her best effort and made love with you.

But then this morning she heard a song on the radio that reminded her that you cheated on her, and her hope now feels futile. The hurt she feels is so deep that she is angry with herself for trusting, hoping, and giving herself to you again.

The whole situation feels supremely unfair to her (which it is), and she is angry that she has to deal with all this. She is thinking:

- "I didn't cheat, and yet I'm stuck having to make the decision whether to stay or leave."
- "I'm a fool for trusting him. He's obviously not happy with me or he wouldn't have cheated. He's just going to leave or cheat again. Why am I even trying?"
- "How can I trust him again? I don't even know him!"

And so she rages at you.

When she blows up, this is what you need to say:

Script:
"I'm so sorry I hurt you this much. I am always here. You take as long as it takes to process this. All I can do is to step up my efforts to rebuild your trust."

I know this might seem counterintuitive, but you saying, "I'm here for you, no matter how long this takes and no matter how angry you may be at me," is the key to shortening the length of the recovery time.

Why does this work? She is still figuring out why you cheated. She wonders if she has to be perfect in order for you to still love her. Remember: Her fear is that you cheated because she isn't good enough for you and that she might be a fool to stay with you. She is afraid of getting hurt even more.

By telling her that you will always be there, you are saying you love her enough to stay with her, even when she isn't perfect. By loving her through her anger, you prove that your love is true.

It shows that you understand this is hard on your wife and you don't expect her to "get over it."

This is also a test. She throws anger at you, like darts. She is testing you to see if you will say, "Forget it. You're not worth it. Too many darts."

You pass the test when you not only stay, but you go so far as to say, "I'll stay forever." This helps to rebuild the intimacy and trust.

When She is Distrustful
There will be times when she ambushes you, insisting on reading emails on your phone, text messages, and posts or messages on your Facebook account. You will need to give her all your passwords and let her have access to all your means of communication so she can check and see that you are no longer in contact with your AP.

She may feel embarrassed or defensive about her insistence on looking at all your private correspondence, and this may come out as anger, with her insisting she has the right to do this. You need to acknowledge her right to this information and hand over all your communication devices humbly and confidently.

Script:
"You have every right to check my correspondence. You are always welcome to look at it, any time you want. You don't even have to ask."

By offering her freedom to check, she will feel more confident that you have nothing to hide. This concept is called "transparency" and will be discussed further in the next chapter.

Accept the Blame When She Vents
Sometimes the crying, anger, or distrust will build to the point that you may feel like she is abusing you.

If she starts calling you names or being especially spiteful, you need to verbalize your willingness to accept all of the blame. You might be tempted to get defensive or tell her that she has also made mistakes, but you will need to resist that temptation. Instead, you can protect yourself (and her) from a damaging fight by carefully diffusing the situation.

Script:
"I know that I have caused you pain. I'm sorry I hurt you. I'm always available to hear that you are angry with me and that what I did was wrong. However, I need a time out from the name calling, so I'm going in the other room."

Then go clean the kitchen, help with the kids, and so on. Make sure to choose an activity that will be obviously edifying to the relationship. You want her to see, if she runs after you, that you are being helpful.

Do NOT get on the computer or text message anyone. This will remind her of you texting and emailing your lover.

Don't watch TV. She will hate you for being selfish and lazy. She will start thinking that even though you aren't perfect, she didn't cheat on you. That will escalate her anger.

Don't hide away in the basement or garage working on a project, either. She will see that as you being selfish (working on something *you* like to do). Deliberately choose something she cannot fault you for doing, like washing the dishes, cooking a meal, or spending time with the kids.

Let's be clear: Much of her anger is to punish you. She wants to hurt you like you have hurt her, but she doesn't think it is possible for you to know the depths of her pain. Therefore, she is going to punish you over and over again.

Also, she is thinking of taking you back, and she wants to make sure that if she does, she won't end up regretting that decision. If she spanks you hard enough, she hopes you'll never do it again.

Finally, she doesn't want you to think she is a doormat for taking you back. She is afraid that she has already lost your respect (after all, she thinks if you had respected her, you wouldn't have cheated on her), and now she needs to regain it. She needs you to know that she is not the type of woman you can walk all over.

Support Her Health
One of the things that I think every single woman coming to my office has said has been the most embarrassing part of the affair is having to go to her doctor and be tested for an STD. She feels like a slut, yet she has been a faithful wife. Her doctor might even suggest she leave you, saying something like, "Once a cheater, always a cheater." Yes, believe me: this actually happens.

Do the right thing. Get tested yourself. Show her the results. If she wants to be tested, ask to go with her. Tell her that you want to be there to tell her doctor that this was all your fault. Tell the doctor that you had an affair, and how since, in addition to the hurt you have caused her, she now has to go through this indignity, you have come to support her. Feel free to well up in tears. Act very remorseful.

This is a powerful gesture for most women. Why? Because she has counted on you as a husband to protect her. When you cheated on her, you stopped protecting her and your marriage. In fact, you hurt her and the marriage.

When you run interference with the doctor, she is no longer at risk of her doctor shaming her or making her feel stupid for staying. You taking the blame is you standing up for her, defending her against feeling shame. It also shows her that you are man enough to humble yourself and take responsibility for what happened.

Support Her Emotional Healing
Whenever you get the chance, you need to connect with your wife emotionally. She needs to feel she is your number one priority, and a great part of that will involve you offering her emotional support—not just regarding the affair, but in all areas of her life. You will want to:

- Hug her often
- Kiss her hello and goodbye every time you can
- Hold her at night
- Cuddle when watching TV at night
- Ask how her day was (and detailed questions thereafter to get her talking)
- Share about your day

In other words, you need connect with her daily, on an emotional level. Give her the emotional support she needs.

You will also need to help her do things that support her

emotional health.

Some suggestions are:

- Give her time to take care of herself by doing more than your fair share of the chores and childcare duties
- Make sure she gets enough sleep
- Cook or bring home healthy groceries so she eats right
- Offer to exercise with her or give her time to exercise (even a simple walk with a friend each day may improve her mood and help her feel more herself)

Be Patient

You probably want this to be over and in the past. You just want to live your life and move forward. However, this may be a lengthy process, and it will take time. If she feels like you are impatient with her, she will be resentful. The process will take even longer. If you are patient and understanding, she will be able to move through this more expediently.

The good days you have together may fool you. However, if you act like everything is better now, she will feel the need to somehow let you know that no, it's not okay already, especially if she feels like you are rushing things. Then she might take a few steps backwards and blow up at you.

Let her know that you understand that just because the two of you are having a good time doesn't mean everything is okay or that your wife isn't thinking about the affair anymore.

Script:

"Thank you for the nice evening. I know that it doesn't mean I have earned your trust, but it makes me hopeful. I want you to know that I understand that you think of what I did all the time. I want you to know that I am also thinking every day about how I can earn your trust back. Thanks again."

By the way, it is not uncommon for your wife to flip out after an amazing time (or even during it). She starts to get comfortable with you again, but then she "catches herself" and needs to protect herself. The script above helps avoid that. She won't feel such a strong need to protect herself and think about it if she knows you are thinking about it. Your verbalization of your awareness allows her to let down her guard.

You will need to work extra hard to create as many good days as possible. That may mean biting your tongue when you normally would have complained, listening more than usual, and in general being on your best behavior. However, your hard work and restraint will pay off. The more good days you put in the bank, the more likely it is that the relationship can be saved.

Chapter Summary: Build, Build, Build... and Then Build Some More

You knew this would be challenging, but presumably you are beginning to understand what is required to rebuild trust. Now that you know what is expected, you can prepare yourself for the long haul. You can also take advantage of this insider knowledge to shorten the duration of this recovery time.

Remember:

- Keep your expectations low.
- Don't demand anything from her.
- Continuously work to rebuild trust and intimacy.
- Show her that you are willing to do anything and everything she needs to rebuild the relationship, no matter how long it takes.

If you take the initiative, you will have a much better chance at rebuilding your marriage. It might even be stronger when you get through this.

Chapter Eight:
Rebuild Trust and Intimacy Through Transparency

You probably already know that she will need you to be more open with her in order for you to rebuild trust in the relationship, but you probably don't realize *how* transparent she will need you to be.

You will need to open up your life completely, because she needs to be shown that you are a person she can trust and admire.

What Exactly Does It Mean to Be Transparent?
Transparency means being on the same team. You're in this together. You have decided to share everything with her, not because you have to, but because you realize that by keeping some things secret, you sabotaged the intimacy in the relationship.

You see, for a while you let your Affair Partner be your closest ally. You put your wife on the outside of the team and let your AP inside, treating her as your closest teammate.

Now that the AP is on the outside and you are opening up to your wife, you are bringing her into your inner circle, and the two of you can become true partners. You form a team. Everyone else is on the outside, and you become truly intimate with your wife because she is on your team.

As you open up to her, she can open up in return, and the two of you can get closer emotionally. The relationship even may be better than ever.

Of course, it goes without saying that you should never tell your wife that the relationship has improved because of the affair. But don't be surprised if she says it to you one day!

Transparency means:

- No secrets
- No hiding anything
- Taking down the walls

This means giving her access to all your accounts—email, cell phone, and Facebook.

You need to show that her you have nothing to hide: You are transparent.

You may think it was the sex with your AP that ruined the relationship, but really, the secrets and lies have damaged the trust in your relationship. She is shaken by the realization that she does not really know you, and she needs to feel like there are no secrets between the two of you. No lies. Only truth. Then she can trust you again.

Extra Bonuses to Being Transparent

As you remove secrets and lies from the relationship, you will find out how good it feels to let someone in that much.

Hopefully by now you realize how much you've devastated her, and *yet she still wants to be with you.*

It's not that she can't get anyone else (because she can).

It's not that she's not strong enough to leave you (because she is).

She is staying with you because *she never stopped loving you.* She loves you unconditionally.

Take a moment and reflect upon how amazing that is. You screwed up this much, and she *still* loves you. She's angry as hell, but she still loves you.

I wanted to point this out because most of the men in my office have told me that they believed their wives had stopped loving them. They didn't feel appreciated or noticed. Their wives never seemed to want sex. Or else, they would have sex but it would feel like a "mercy screw" and not like she was into it.

A common sentiment men have shared with me is: "It's not that my AP was hotter or younger. I just felt like she truly liked me."

Well, now you've found out the truth: Your wife really does love you after all.

This is why a relationship is often better after an affair. You finally take down your protective walls and hurt and are able to be really close to your wife. As you open up all the way, and she does the same, you will find that the walls you've built between you will fall, and you will be closer than you ever imagined you could be. You will feel like you're on the same team again.

How Transparency Heals PTAS

Every time your wife checks your email or cell phone and sees that you are not doing anything shady, you will help her start to heal. Every time you text to let her know where you are or to invite her to join you, she will feel a little less guarded. These repeated acts of transparency will help her feel less traumatized and more like she can relax and stop worrying that you will blindside her again. She will start building up a belief that you are trustworthy.

Know that her flashbacks of you cheating on her will happen less and less frequently and dwindle to shorter duration as time passes (assuming you've taken actions to help her move through this instead of hurting her again and again). Eventually the affair will not weigh on her mind on a daily basis.

However, there may be certain issues that will always trigger her to feel emotional or suspicious. For example, if you cheated while you were out of town, you might have to call in every night that you're out of town on business for the rest of your marriage. Overall, it will get better—if you keep opening up and offering the full truth, again, and again, and again.

How to Be Transparent

You will need to become transparent with your schedule and where you are. If you keep an electronic calendar, you may wish to give her access to it so she knows where you will be and what you are doing at all times. Then, when your plans change, you will need to let her know about changes.

For example: If you say you are going to Vons but you actually go to Whole Foods, text your wife as soon as you know, *before* you go to the different store.

Seems ridiculous, doesn't it? Until a friend of your wife says to her, "I saw your husband at Whole Foods. Aren't you lucky you have a man who shops?"

All she hears is: "You lied about where you were! What else are you lying about? Does [your Affair Partner] live nearby? Is that why you switched stores and didn't tell me?"

You can avoid any such incident by simply shooting off a quick text to her saying, "Honey, have to go to Whole Foods; Vons didn't have the gourmet olives after all."

Sure, she might think, "Why the hell is he texting me this stupid stuff?" But trust me, within a few seconds she will think, "Oh, I guess he 'gets it'. I don't trust him, and he wants to reassure me."

Every time you reassure her like this, it will rebuild her trust a little.

Make sure you:

- Always text her to let her know if you'll be late and to explain why.
- Reply to her emails, messages, or calls right away so she never worries that you are unavailable because you are with your AP and so she feels prioritized.
- Let her know who you are with and where you will be at all times.

Your transparency will help her believe you are truly all hers again. She needs to believe she can trust you and that she is not sharing you with anyone else.

What to Do if Your Affair Partner Contacts You

This is exactly what your wife fears most of all: that your AP will contact you, you will secretly start the relationship back up again, and she will get hurt even worse than she already was.

This is why you have to handle this situation the right way.

If you get an email, text, or some form of initiation from your AP, tell your wife right away.

Why? Because you will lose everything if you hide this from your wife and she later finds out the truth.

I always tell my clients, "Take the hit in the short term." Don't "protect her" from this information. I know that you're thinking: "Why rock the boat when my wife has nothing to worry about?"

DO NOT DO THIS. Your wife will sense that you are withholding something from her (and therefore imagine worse things). If she finds out (and remember she probably will—she is watching your every move right now), all she will see is that you are again communicating with your AP behind her back. This, on many occasions, is what has caused a divorce. Again,

IT IS NOT THE AFFAIR ITSELF THAT CAUSED THE DIVORCE. The wife gave up trying when the husband continued to be selfish, shady, and untrustworthy.

Script:
"I know that this is a painful reminder of what I did, but I wanted you to know [AP's name] contacted me. My thought is to not respond to her, but what is it that *you* think *our* response should be to her?"

Your wife might get angry. In fact, she might get VERY angry. But you know what? She has registered the following:

- You have come home to her. The two of you are a team and your AP is on the OUTSIDE.
- It was difficult for you to bring this to her. You must be really trying to work on the marriage if you were willing to reveal this.
- She is relieved that she didn't have to uncover it or pry it out of you. She is angry in the short term, but she is beginning to feel safe with you again.

If your AP contacts you, and you hide or delete evidence of that contact, and then your wife somehow finds out, this will be your *nuclear winter*.

I always tell my clients this. Unfortunately, some of them choose not to follow my advice. Then the wife ends up seeing something and goes absolutely ballistic. I've worked with couples for months who were in such a good place, but then the wife uncovered a new hidden contact. BOOM! **Divorce**.

Why? Because she finally had gone all in and put her trust back into her husband. Most times the marriage is better. Then she finds the information and feels like a fool. "Fool me once, shame on *you*; fool me twice, shame on *me*." She feels like a complete moron for trusting you. It is next to impossible for you to recover from that.

Who to Tell/Not to Tell

Part of being transparent is also being willing to discuss what happened with the people your wife wants to involve. For example, she may want to work through this with the help of clergy or a therapist. She may also want you to tell certain people, like her parents. This can get tricky, because she may want to force you to confess to people who really should not get involved or find out. However, you need to respect her feelings about who she wants to tell. The fewer people who know, the better. Even if you are able to heal your marriage, it will be difficult to reintegrate into your social group or her family when everyone knows your marriage was in trouble.

Your wife may feel the need to tell someone what happened as part of her healing process. If she has to pretend with everyone that nothing happened, she may feel that this is an unfair burden for her to bear. After all, she isn't the one who cheated, and yet she's the one who is hurting the most. The following are examples of people wives often want to tell and how you should handle each situation.

The Children

The children should **<u>not</u>** be told if they don't know yet. **This is the hill you should die on.** If you tell them, you will involve them in deep adult issues that will threaten their foundation for all relationships. It will cause them to worry and wonder if they can ever really trust their future romantic partner.

This is the case even if your child is an adult. It will affect your relationship with them as their father. They won't know how to feel about you. They will naturally want to protect their mother. But sons and daughters need their fathers just as much as they need their mothers.

Do not let your affair be known to your children. If they have figured out something is awry, offer to tell them something like, "Daddy hurt Mommy's feelings. Mommy has good reason to be mad at Daddy."

If she still wants to tell them, tell her you would like the advice of a professional on how to handle this. Hopefully, a professional will be able to talk some sense into her.

Your In-Laws
Has your wife already told her parents?

If she has told her parents, then yes, you must have a conversation with them. You cheated on their daughter. My advice is to go with your wife to meet with them in person and let them know you understand that your decision also hurt them and their trust in you. But go together as a couple, as a united front. Do not be afraid to cry or well up with tears. Let them know you realize that you almost lost everything.

Men, if you took the traditional approach and you asked her father for her hand in marriage, then you will have to go a step further and talk to her father directly. Yes, he hates you and wants to kick your ass. *If you have a daughter, you know just how much.*

Script:
"I know I asked for your daughter's hand X many years ago. You said 'yes', believing that I would cherish and protect her. You never would have said 'yes' if you knew that I would hurt your daughter this way.

"Please know I understand that in addition to trying to rebuild the trust with her, I owe an apology to you directly for dishonoring my word to you. I understand if you never forgive me, but please know that I will spend the rest of my life trying to make this up to your daughter, and I will never do this again."

If She Hasn't Told Her Parents
If your wife hasn't told her parents, chances are it's because she's not only embarrassed, but she's also afraid that if she tells

her parents, they will not support her decision to stay married to you. She doesn't want to look weak. She also doesn't want to cause complications with you and them until she's made a decision that she is leaving you. Do not bring up telling her parents. If she wonders aloud whether she should, be prepared with the right thing to say.

Script:
"It is, of course, up to you. I broke your family's trust. If you would like me to meet with them to confess what I have done and accept responsibility for this, I will. I do worry that if you decide to stay married to me and they know about this, it will be difficult for them to see me at holidays like Thanksgiving. It would make things awkward for them."

Chances are: If she hasn't told yet, she isn't telling. You get the brownie points for offering to man up.

Your Affair Partner's Husband
At some point your wife might be so angry that she says she wants to tell your Affair Partner's husband that she cheated on him (if she is also married or in a relationship). She will say that she wants to ruin her marriage the way your AP ruined hers.

If you don't care whether or not your AP's husband knows, then let your wife decide.

If you do care whether your AP's husband knows, then you have to handle this situation very carefully. You cannot come across in any way that sounds like you are defending or protecting your AP. You have to phrase it as if you're making this choice to protect another victim of the affair, your AP's husband. Yes, he is a victim in this, too.

Script:
"I support whatever decision you make; I have no right to tell you what to do or what not to do. I know you're angry now, but

please think of her husband. I understand wanting revenge on her, but he hasn't done anything wrong here. The affair is over. He is no longer in jeopardy."

If she says, "He should know out of 'fairness' to him."

Script:
"I ask you to take a look at this closely to determine if you want to tell him because you really think he should know or if it's because you want to get revenge. I have hurt our marriage so much already, and I worry that telling him might complicate things for you and me recovering from this."

You could also say the following.

Script:
"I cry when I think of the hurt and devastation my actions have caused you. I would hate to bring that level of hurt upon another person."

Finally:
"There is a real possibility that he may come over here with a gun. I worry that saying something to him will put our lives in jeopardy."

Rebuilding Sexual Intimacy
Different wives respond differently to discovering their husband has had an affair. Some shut down sexually, refusing to engage in sexual intimacy for a long time. Some choose to punish their husbands by withholding sex until they feel vindicated. Some offer sex when they feel close and then withdraw again when they experience a powerful PTAS trigger.

You probably expected to hear all of those actions. However, when certain women find out their husband has cheated, they respond by wanting more sex. Why? Your wife may realize she wasn't engaging with you enough sexually, or she may believe it is her fault that you strayed. Some women want to have sex as a way to heal the relationship again.

If this happens to you, you are a very lucky man.

It is important that you don't do or say anything suggesting you think that since you cheated, you are getting more sex. Instead, do things like talk to her more. Buy her flowers. Let her feel wooed by you.

Other women naturally don't want to have sex because they don't trust you anymore. All I can say is take it slow. Embrace every gesture of hers to move forward.

Some tips for rebuilding sexual intimacy with your wife:

- Be patient if she is not ready to have sex with you yet.
- Spend plenty of time cuddling with her without making a move towards sex. She needs to be comforted, loved, snuggled, and assured that she is safe with you.
- Don't turn her down if she initiates. Your answer must always be an enthusiastic and grateful "yes."
- Prioritize her pleasure at all times. Take your time, pay attention to what gives her pleasure, and make sure you do what she wants, not what you want.
- Be careful not to do anything that will remind her that you were with someone else. If you learned some new move or position from your AP, you cannot try it on her. If she accuses you of doing something differently and gets upset because she is reminded of your AP, stop trying to make love to her and instead focus completely on comforting her and assuring her it's just you and her in the bedroom. Nobody else.
- Hold her afterwards. No more rolling over and going to sleep or getting up to go do something else. Make sure she feels loved and appreciated.

This is a critical part of your relationship, so you need to pour yourself into repairing this. Do not get discouraged if it takes a while. Just persevere and offer up as much kindness and love as you can.

Chapter Summary: Building Trust and Intimacy

Remember, if you want to repair the relationship (and even make it better than before), you will need to:

- Open up
- Communicate daily about where you are and who you are with
- Let her check in on your email, text messages, etc. as much as she needs
- Pull her into your inner circle (and keep your AP out)
- Talk to the people she feels need an explanation
- Embrace sexual intimacy at her pace

If you do these things, you will rebuild her trust and develop intimacy with your wife. This is key to moving past the affair and building a loving marriage.

Chapter Nine: Infidelity Relapse Prevention

Your wife's biggest fear is that you will relapse into the relationship with your Affair Partner. This should be your biggest fear as well, because you probably won't get another chance if you do. Because here is the truth: She will believe once that you really didn't understand that it would hurt her. But now that you do know, if you have another affair, she will believe that you are cruel and don't love her.

Then she will walk.

And hate you forever.

I know you might miss your AP. I know it's tempting to get back together with her, and you may want to justify this with thoughts like, "We need closure," or "We didn't get to say a true goodbye." However, meeting up with your AP will most likely open the door for yet more involvement. Seeing your AP will rekindle feelings and dull you to the emotional connection to your wife. It may even make you forget how sorry you were when you realized how much you hurt your wife.

Right now your marriage is incredibly vulnerable. At this moment, you are finally reconnecting with your wife. You are in touch with how she feels, and you actually care how much your infidelity hurt her. If you turn that emotional connection off and reinvest in your AP again, you will probably break your marriage forever.

It bears repeating: Contact with your AP is as dangerous to your marriage as heroin is to a junkie. Like a junkie can't have just a little smack of heroin, you can't just have a little contact with your former AP.

This is a precious time. You need to act to rebuild your relationship with your wife now, while you are 100% invested in her, and you need to keep your AP out. You also need to figure out some things so that you can affair-proof your marriage for the future.

Preparing for Contact From Your Ex-AP

You know your AP well, so you probably can anticipate if she will contact you or not. You also can probably guess how she might contact you.

If you had a short, sexual fling, you might be lucky. She might be able to just move on. However, if you fell in love, and even talked about a future together, she will probably be crushed and depressed at the ending of your affair. She might contact you—maybe even multiple times and in multiple ways, trying to get back together.

She will probably say things like:

- "I need to see you once more to have a proper goodbye."
- "I just need to talk to you so I can get closure."
- "You used me and then just dumped me. What kind of an jerk does that? You *owe* me a proper goodbye."
- "You said you weren't happy with your wife. And now you're choosing her over me?"
- "We can just be friends. Isn't our friendship valuable to you?"

The Plan

When she contacts you by email, text, or voicemail, you need to not reply until you've talked to your wife (as discussed earlier). Then respond as your wife sees fit: with either silence or a short, terse response you and your wife crafted together.

The response should say something like this:

"I'm sorry this is hard for you, but I can no longer have any contact with you at all. I am rededicating myself to my marriage. If you contact me again, I will not reply at all."

The bottom line is this: You cannot be in contact with her any longer. I know this might be difficult for you. Again, I urge you to see an individual therapist if you need to work through your feelings of loss, guilt, and depression. This will help you stay strong through a very hard time.

Why Did I Do This?

A lot of men tell me they aren't sure why they decided to cheat. Now that they've been exposed, they look back at their decisions and wonder how they ever could have minimized their actions. They may be tempted to want the focus to be on them, exploring why they cheated and what that says about them.

This is fine—as long as you limit your focus on yourself to individual therapy sessions, in which I strongly encourage you to indulge. You need a place to explore the following:

- What is the root cause of your infidelity?
- How much of the reason has to do with problems inside the marriage, and how much of the reason is rooted in your own emotional and psychological needs (for adventure, excitement, sexual pleasure, admiration, respect, etc.)?
- What marriage vulnerabilities have existed and still exist?
- Why did you feel that it was acceptable to go outside of the marriage to get your needs met? Why did you feel like you couldn't get your needs met inside the confines of your marriage?

Whereas it's tempting to blame everything on your wife (she didn't do this, she didn't do that), it's very possible that your infidelity is rooted in a psychological need you have. Perhaps you don't feel attractive enough, and as such, you are vulnerable to women who make you feel sexy and appealing. Maybe you have a need for adventure and excitement, and sex outside of marriage gave you that thrill.

Or maybe the problem really is due to unmet needs in your marriage. Maybe your wife hasn't been into sex, and you feel sexually deprived or disappointed. Maybe your wife isn't very complimentary, and you needed to be built up and respected.

Whatever the reasons, you need to identify what they are and then come up with a plan for dealing with them. If you ignore this piece of the puzzle, you will probably cheat again.

Common Reasons Men Cheat
You need to understand why you cheated so you can make lasting changes.

At the end of the book there are two quizzes, "**What Kind of Affair Did I Have?**" and "**Sexual Addiction Self-Assessment**." Please take both of them now.

At some point in the future, you will need to share with your wife why you think the relationship was vulnerable and why you crossed that line.

However, you will need to do this later, after the relationship has been firmly re-established. In the beginning, she will be hypersensitive any signs that you blame her for the affair. You will need to wait until the relationship is solid again. She needs to feel safe before she can delve into this with you.

Set aside time to explore this and deal with your emotions associated with this personal topic. Then you will be ready to work through these issues with her when the time comes, without needing to defend yourself too much.

Preventing a Relapse or a New Affair
Now that you know that you are vulnerable to having an affair, you need to think of this as your Achilles heel. This is your weakness, and you need to work to prevent yourself from ever cheating again.

There are several common vulnerabilities for which a man has to watch. I have found Peggy Vaughan's book, *The Monogamy Myth* (1989), to be inspiring, and I have combined some of her theories with my own strategies for helping men stay faithful to their wives.

The following are some of the issues I advise the men in my office to educate themselves about and then protect themselves against.

Beware of the Common Infidelity Door Openers

You have proven to be vulnerable to having an affair, so you need to be aware of infidelity door openers and avoid the following tempting situations and/or relationships:

Platonic Friendships With Women
Let's face it: A lot of men and women have trouble "just being friends." You may face ridicule, but you need to limit any friendships you have with women. Friendships become dangerous when you:

- Start sharing emotionally intimate information, even stuff as benign as how frustrated you feel with work or how angry you get when your wife doesn't clean out the cat box
- Begin telling your female friend about things that are emotionally important to you—especially if you start telling her details you are not telling your wife
- Spending time together
- Touching, even in non-erogenous zones

If you have a female friend who means a lot to you, the friendship needs to become a three-way friendship, with your wife being just as involved as you are. Your wife needs to be copied on emails, and coffee dates should include your wife. No more going to the game with your friend Suzy just because Suzy likes basketball and your wife doesn't. Either replace Suzy with a male friend, or bring your wife along—and have her sit between you and Suzy.

Work Relationships
A large percentage of affairs happen in the workplace. Why? Because women and men working together get to know each other on a somewhat intimate level. You get to know her likes and dislikes, you can have lunch together, or you work on a project together and experience the ups and downs of the success or failure of that project. You see each other regularly, meaning you get a idea of who she really is.

That familiarity breeds comfort. As your comfort level grows, you start to share more and more of who you are—especially if she is attentive, respectful, and admiring. Add in travel for work and you've got extra opportunity in the mix.

This can quickly turn into an affair.

You will need to keep all work relationships with women to a minimum. Some men need to see a therapist ongoing so as to confide in the therapist when he feels attracted to a woman, and to get support placing appropriate boundaries.

Relatives and Family Friends
Believe or not, a large percentage of affairs happen with wives' relatives and family friends. Like work relationships, these are women you get to know well. They have a built-in excuse to spend time with you—after all, you're family!

You have plenty of opportunities to show off your skills and positive attributes, and meanwhile, so does she—all in the context of accepted interactions, many of which are rather intimate. Maybe you like the way your sister-in-law admires you as you comfort your infant son, or you find yourself showing off as you install a new deck in front of your wife's best friend. She gets to see you doing things she admires, and you feel flattered as she tells you how awesome you are...
You will need to establish boundaries with all of your female relatives and family friends, especially those you find attractive or admirable.

Internet

You may be tempted to roll your eyes at the mention of the big bad internet as a risk factor, but cybersex, internet relationships, and "catching up" with an old flame online can quickly turn into affair. The internet provides several of the factors necessary to develop an affair: secrecy, the ability to present only your best features, and plenty of room for fantasy.

But you've lost your right to privacy with the internet. You will want to move your computer to the main family room and only use it in front of your wife, not alone in secret. Offer her the password to be the administrator of the computer, and let her browse your history at any time. You need to protect yourself—and her—from any inappropriate online behavior.

** A Note About Porn

Even the most open-minded wife will now feel threatened by you looking at porn, trolling Craigslist, or chatting online with another woman. You have already shown through your actions that your wife wasn't "enough" for you. Please don't remind her of that.

Basically, you need to protect yourself from temptation on all fronts. If you need assistance, see an individual therapist on a regular basis to get the support you need.

Emotional & Psychological Issues That Open the Door to an Affair

You will want to look into your own emotional and psychological needs to determine what made you vulnerable to having an affair. The following are common issues I see with men in my office.

Lack of Boundaries

If you are an oversharer, or someone who touches other people a lot, you may not have recognized the fact that you were crossing boundaries until you were in too deep. You will need to learn how to avoid infidelity denial—in other words, how to identify where boundaries should be. Ask yourself: When did you know it was going too far? Why did you cross that line once you knew you were on the brink?

Ego Gratification

Let's face it: having a lover probably made you feel great. You felt desired and admired. You felt powerful. You probably felt a bit invincible, or like you "had it all"—a wife, a lover. You probably bought into the societal message that says that a man is successful if multiple women desire him.

Many men who need to feel admired, respected, or desired are vulnerable to affairs. If you need your ego stroked, then find healthier ways to get this need met.

Desensitization

Perhaps your parents had affairs or your coworkers have had affairs, and this knowledge made it not seem so bad. We see affairs glorified in the media, which can make you feel like it's not such a big deal. Hopefully you now see how destructive an affair is and will be motivated never to indulge again.

The Idea That Ignorance is Bliss

You may have bought into the idea that what your wife doesn't know won't hurt her. Well, she did find out, and it has hurt her—tremendously.

Now it's time to take inventory of what you lost. You spent time away from work, home, and the kids. You spent money and your emotional energy on your AP instead of your marriage. You poured your heart and attention into this other woman, and now you don't even know if your most valuable relationship can be saved.

Promise yourself that you will never buy into this thinking again.

Chapter Summary: You Were Unhappy, Miserable, and Didn't See Any Hope That it Would Get Better

Nothing your wife did made her deserve this, but there might have been things within the relationship that made it vulnerable. You need to identify what issues made you unhappy and made you look outside the marriage to get your needs met. Then you need to express to your wife what you need in the relationship and find out if she can be the partner you need.

This is when professional relationship counseling can help. Once you get your relationship stable enough to handle couples counseling, I strongly suggest you see a pro-marriage counselor together to shore up the areas of vulnerability.

Chapter Ten: Other Situations

Some of you are dealing with situations not yet discussed in this book. Perhaps you had an emotional affair, and you wonder why your wife is so upset when you feel like you haven't really done anything wrong yet. Or perhaps you've had an affair, but your wife has not discovered this yet, and you're wondering what to do. This last chapter covers these issues.

Situation #1:
My Wife Doesn't Know About the Affair.
Should I Tell Her?

Some of you may be reading this book because you have had an affair, but you haven't gotten caught yet, and you are trying to figure out how to tell her the right way.

If this is your situation, I have some tried and true advice that may surprise you.

I'll start with the bad news: the situations in which you absolutely MUST tell her you strayed. If you find yourself in one of these three scenarios, you have no choice but to come clean.

1. You contracted an STD from your Affair Partner.
If your doctor says you have contracted something and that you should tell your romantic partners, then don't play doctor and decide that you don't have to tell your wife.

Here's the thing: Even if the STD with which you were initially diagnosed was treatable with some antibiotics, you really don't know what else you might have. What else does your AP have? Many STDs are asymptomatic, meaning you might not have (or recognize) the symptoms, and you may pass on something that will seriously affect your wife's health.

For example: Men often don't show signs of genital warts. Genital warts have been shown to lead to cervical cancer in women. If your wife is pregnant or nursing, not telling her could have *devastating* effects on your child.

Conclusion: Get a full STD panel test, including a test for herpes simplex II (you have to ask for this test specifically—it costs extra and is not included in the standard screening), because over 75% of the people who contract herpes are asymptomatic. If you have contracted something, then man up and tell your wife.

2. You have gotten your Affair Partner pregnant and she is going to have the baby.

Wow. That's tough, brother. I want to acknowledge how difficult this situation is.

However, my opinion is that you always have to protect children. *All* children. Your AP's child has an equal right to have you as a father. Not just your money. *You.*

Worried about how this will affect the children you have with your wife? Your other children will find out one day anyhow, even if it's not until they're adults. Your kids won't think you are an honorable man if you kept their half-sibling in the closet.

I know you are probably looking for ways to get around this mess, but you need to face the following facts:

That promise that your AP will keep the child a secret won't hold.

Your AP might say that she'll keep it a secret, but let me tell you the truth: *That* promise will only last until the two of you have a falling out. Then she will take you to court for child support. Or blackmail you. Friend, those scenarios aren't *Tales from the Crypt* horror stories; they are *Tales from My Therapy Couch* real-life scenarios.

Your wife will lose all respect for you when she finds out you tried to hide or abandon a child.

Don't fool yourself. I always tell my male clients: "Stop thinking like a man, because your wife ain't no man!" Once your wife finds out (and trust me, she will someday), she will think that not only are you a cheater, but that you are also a man who would abandon his own child for convenience.

She won't be fooled into believing you hid your love child to "protect" her feelings. First of all, she thinks if you cared about her feelings you wouldn't have cheated in the first place. But this is the bottom line: Women can sometimes get over the fact that their husband had sex with another woman. However, she will struggle more with the betrayal of trust, not the fact that you thought with the wrong head.

Remember, she is a woman. She doesn't think like you. The most abhorrent thing for a normal mother is the thought of abandoning a child. It is part of a woman's DNA to die and kill for her children. Denying the existence of your child is more likely to be the unforgivable offense, not the affair. (No, she won't like it and might not embrace your AP's child, but your wife will think worse of you if you abandon the kid.)

Conclusion: If you want to save this relationship, you have to come clean about the affair and the child.

3. You know someone else knows about the affair and is about to expose you.

I don't mean to say you should tell her if you are scared and nervous that someone *might* tell her. You should only tell her if you know *for sure* that someone is about to tell her.

By the way, can you guess who is the most likely person to tell on you?

Her sister?
Her best friend?

Nope. They won't want to get involved. **YOUR AFFAIR PARTNER** is the one who is most likely to tell your wife.

But if you are sure your wife will hear about the affair from someone, make sure she hears it from you. If you come clean before someone else tells her, you have a much better chance of regaining her trust and saving the relationship.

Conclusion: Tell your wife NOW before someone else tells her and takes away your chance to do the "right thing."

What If I'm Not in One of Those Three Situations? Shouldn't I Confess Anyway?

There are a lot of people who have strong opinions about this subject. They like to stand on their soapboxes, telling you that you have to confess if you have any integrity at all. People like to say things like, "She has the right to know so she can make an informed decision," or, "You're not really sorry if you don't own up to your infidelity and take her response like a man."

However, we live in the real world, not an idyllic one. This isn't about whether or not it is fair to withhold the truth from your wife. It's also not about whether you can handle the punishment she's bound to inflict upon you if you confess. This is about what will help you save your relationship (assuming that's what you want), and the reality of the situation is this: Confessing usually hurts the relationship more than it helps it.

Stop and think about this for a moment. What wife *wants* to know her husband cheated on her? What wife responds positively to finding out her husband has betrayed her?

"Thanks for devastating my world by telling me you cheated on me. Now I am left with two horrible options: either divorce you even though I *was* happy in this marriage, or stay with you knowing that you are a cheater," said no wife, ever. Confessing is not the way to save a marriage. End of story. Let me explain why.

Why You Should Not Tell Your Wife You've Had an Affair

The men in my office usually have one of two reasons why they want to tell their wife they had an affair.

Reason One: You want to feel close to her.

After a rough patch with your wife, the two of you are in a better place. In order to move forward in the relationship, you want there to be no secrets between you and no walls. You believe that you cannot be emotionally close to her unless you confess.

Why is confession a terrible idea? Simply put: because the exposure of your affair will cause such a deep level of devastation that you will jeopardize your relationship entirely.

You may think confessing will deepen the relationship, when ironically it might end it. She won't think your disclosure is an amazing act of togetherness and love. She won't rejoice that she can now get closer to you because now there are no secrets.

She will just hear that you cheated on her. It doesn't matter if it was years ago. (Actually, that can make it worse, because now she realizes you've been lying to her face for *years*.)

She will think:

"We were finally in a good place. I thought we had made it together through a rough patch as a team. But *we* didn't. *He* left when things got bad."

You basically have given her the worst horror movie of her life, a film that will replay in her head forever. She will look back at all those "happy photos" of the two of you and realize that in the picture she was smiling like a fool. A fool whose husband cheated on her, and she didn't even know.

Worse yet, she will think you aren't really over your lover. She will wonder, "Why is he telling me this? If it is truly over and he has recommitted to our marriage, why is he telling me at all?"

Reason Two: Your conscience is killing you.
Do you feel guilty? Well, you *should* feel guilty. What you did was selfish. Now don't make it worse by telling her. Suck it up.

What good will it do for you to tell her? It will only hurt her. Tremendously. Telling her just to relieve your conscience is another selfish act that hurts her and benefits only you.

If you feel guilty about your affair, make an appointment with a therapist or pastoral counselor and start working through your issues on your own. End it with the AP and figure out if the relationship will work without your wife's knowledge of the affair.

When the guilt and remorse hit you, channel those feelings into doing something nice for your wife. Use the guilt to make yourself a better husband.

Make a promise to yourself that if you are tempted to cheat again, you won't. You won't use the fact that you "got away with it" to deceive your wife again. Go to marriage counseling or divorce her. Otherwise, you are not a good man who made a poor choice. You are a just a *cheater*.

If you've had an affair and now regret it, I feel for you. You've made a poor choice, but you can't go back and undo what has already been done. However, you can make wise decisions as you move forward and try to repair the relationship.

The affair should be a red flag for you. If you still want your marriage, end things with your Affair Partner.

Important Tip: End it with your AP nicely. If you and your wife have kids, mention the kids as the top reason you have to end the affair. You don't want your AP to get angry and tell your wife (which APs have been known to do). Delete all emails, pictures, texts, and secret accounts. Do not keep anything that reminds you of your AP. Nothing that is a "souvenir" or anything else that will cause you to pine over her in a weak moment. Tell yourself that it is over.

Give it two weeks.

Then sit your wife down and tell her in no uncertain terms that you are unhappy and seriously considering divorce (not in a heated argument, but calmly). Suggest couples counseling or meeting with clergy. She may assume at this point that you are having an affair and will check email, text messages, Facebook, and the cell phone bill (possibly yet another reason to delete your AP from your life). You want counseling to be about fixing the marriage, not recovering from the affair.

P.S. See a pro-marriage therapist.

P.P.S. If you still question my advice, read chapter 3 about how the discovery of an affair affects wives.

*P.P.P.S. The rest of the men reading this book think you have no clue how **bad** of an idea it is for you to tell your wife. They would do anything to be you and to be able to just stop the affair and never have their wives know what happened.*

Situation #2:
What If We're Not Actually Married Yet?

Notice that throughout this book I use the terms "marriage," "husband," and "wife"? I do this on purpose. If you are married, at some point you made a decision that your wife was "the one." You may have grown apart, but at one point you were confident enough to say to the world that you were ready to commit to this one woman for the rest of your life.

Some of you are reading this book but you aren't married. You are in a serious, committed relationship; maybe you even live together. However, you have cheated on her, and now you're wondering if maybe she isn't "the one."

Now, I'm not saying your AP was "the one." I'm saying: If you haven't felt strongly enough to put a ring on your girlfriend's finger AND you've cheated on her, you need to take a look at that.

I think that if you have kids together, you should work hard on seeing if the relationship is salvageable in order to spare the kids. But no kids? No marriage? Then maybe the affair has revealed something your heart knew already.

Situation #3:
But It Didn't Even Get Physical!
How to Handle an Emotional Affair

If you were caught in an emotional affair, you may be puzzled as to why your wife is responding the way she is.

I know that you're thinking, "With all the aggravation I'm getting over this, I should have slept with her!" No, had you actually slept with your AP, you would be in a divorce attorney's office! You need to treat this as a serious breach. You could have gone through with it, and your wife knows it. And she thinks that if she hadn't found out, the affair would have continued.

Why does an emotional affair bother your wife so much? Sociologists tell us that men and women bond with each other in different ways. However, we all bond for the same reason: We each act in ways that will best allow us to procreate and carry on our genes.

So what does this mean? As a man, you instinctively want your wife to be faithful so you are sure that the offspring for whom you provide are yours. A woman obviously knows the children are hers. Women want to create an emotional bond and be a good partner to the man they've chosen to be with so their children will have the resources they need to carry on their genes.

This is why women are more upset by emotional infidelity— *"Did you love her?"*

And men are more upset by sexual infidelity—*"Did you sleep with him?"*

Even if you don't "get" this piece of the puzzle, you'll need to accept it as her truth. Your emotional infidelity is just as painful to her as sexual infidelity would be to you.

The point is this: if you don't take this seriously and instead try to impose your (male) viewpoint on your wife because you don't think the affair was a big deal (because you didn't sleep with her), you will get into trouble.

Many men in my office have said things like:

- "Get over it."
- "I should have slept with her."
- "What's the big deal?"
- "You have male friends; stop talking to them."

If you treat the emotional affair like it's not a big deal, she gets stuck feeling like you don't get it. She thinks: "If you don't think it's a big deal, you will do it again."

You've got to convince her that you DO get it and that you won't do it again because you understand how much it hurt her.

Coming Clean About an Emotional Affair

Coming clean about an emotional affair can be tricky. You have to acknowledge that what you did was wrong and outside the boundaries, but you can't act so guilty that she thinks you actually had sex. It is a difficult tightrope to walk.

The first thing you need to understand is that your wife is not sure you didn't have a physical affair. You need to convince her that you did not sleep with your AP.

How can you do this? Come clean with everything. You need to show her all the emails and all the secret Facebook messages you sent to each other so she will see that you didn't have a hotel room booked and that there were no discussions about how great the sex was, etc.

Script:
"I know that it didn't have to be a physical affair to violate your trust in me. I consider this an affair, too. It is a big deal that I flirted with another woman, even if we didn't have physical contact."

Point: You are sorry. However, you didn't sleep with her!

The following question will inevitably come up:

Q: "If I hadn't had caught you, would the affair have progressed to a physical contact?"

Script:
"Thank God we'll never know because the affair was revealed before it went that far. I can say that I don't believe so. I have to believe that when I got to the point of physically crossing the line, the reality of what I was doing would have hit me, and I would have stopped myself. I think at the time I felt like it was harmless flirting. It inflated my ego and made me feel good about myself."

Chapter Summary: Openness and Humility Are Key, Regardless of Your Situation

Remember: Openness and humility are the keys to winning back her trust. The more open you are, the more likely she is to trust you in the long run, even if the things you disclose to her now are painful and embarrassing.

Conclusion: Show Her That You Are, In Fact, a Good Man Who Made a Bad Choice

Do not hide the fact that you are reading this book from your wife. The more she knows that you are indeed a good man who made a bad decision, the more confident she can feel that she can trust you again. Good people do make bad decisions that they regret. She does, in her heart, know who you really are. She is just understandably confused now because of your actions.

Let her know that you are reading this book. Then let her *see* you reading this book, highlighting sections, and tell her, "This is helping me better understand how my actions hurt you, and I will never do this again."

Despite the common belief that a relationship cannot survive an affair, you now know that it is possible to save your marriage after infidelity. The first weeks and months are most important, so you will need to devote yourself to repairing the relationship during this time. Follow my advice, and you might be able to get your wife to trust you again.

In a nutshell, you will need to:

- Show her that you "get" her pain
- Apologize repeatedly
- Promise to never cheat again
- Take responsibility

- Prove to her that you are worthy of her trust by changing your behavior
- Come clean with everything
- Become transparent
- Take care of her in her time of need

If you truly want to save your marriage, put these simple practices into action. Give your wife time, and continue to show her (through both words and actions) that you have returned to her, wholeheartedly and with total commitment.

It is my hope that you will win your wife back and that the two of you will find ways to make your relationship even better than it has ever been.

Wishing you the best,

Dr. Caroline Madden
Licensed Marriage & Family Therapist

Resources

In this section, I have provided several resources that I hope will prove helpful to you. You will find a quiz titled "What Type of Affair Did I Have?", a Sexual Addiction Self-Assessment quiz, citations to works either cited or used for inspiration, and a list of recommended reading materials. I hope you find these resources helpful.

Diagnostic Quiz: What Kind of Affair Did I Have?

To determine what type of affair you had, answer yes or no to the following questions. Then compare your answers to those listed in the different affair types listed below. Your answers may point to more than one affair. Your affair type will be the one where you answer the most questions in relation to that type.

1. Do you and your wife fight a lot?
2. Was it easy for you to end the affair?
3. Are you tempted to go back to your AP?
4. Have you talked to your wife about your needs and wants in the relationship, yet still feel she is unwilling to help you meet them?
5. Do you feel emotionally distant from your wife and kids?
6. Do you think you should be able to have everything you want in life?
7. Was your affair a one-night stand?
8. Do you desire to end your marriage?
9. Do you avoid talking to your partner about problems that may lead to disagreements?
10. Do you feel guilty about having an affair?
11. Are you generally a risk taker?
12. Do you lie to avoid unpleasant things, not just in your marriage, but in different parts of your life?

13. Have you cut most or all emotional ties to your marriage?
14. Has your spouse also had an affair?
15. Have you made a lot of personal sacrifices to try to make your marriage work?
16. Was your affair unplanned and spontaneous?
17. Do you try to be emotionally engaged and actively involved with your wife and children?
18. Was this a short term affair (less than 6 months)?
19. Do you feel ambivalent about ending your marriage, even if you have decided that you want to do so?
20. Did your affair happen due to unusual events, such as travel, drugs, or alcohol, which normally aren't an issue in your relationship?
21. Is your biggest fear that of being discovered?
22. Was your AP a friend before you started cheating with her?

Types of Affairs

The Conflict Avoidance Affair:

If you answered NO to question 1 and YES to questions 2, 9, 10, and 18, you fit this type.

You do everything possible to avoid fighting with your wife. You don't want to hurt her feelings and don't want to get into conflict with her.

You fear that your wife will abandon you or otherwise hurt you if you express or admit your needs. You may even struggle with disagreeing with your wife and feel like you constantly make concessions to keep the peace.

Because of this, you don't tell your wife what you need and want for fear of upsetting her. You had an affair to get your needs met that you feared your wife would not meet. You tend to have short-term affairs and are not emotionally attached to your AP because your primary motivation for the affair is to get specific needs met and to avoid conflict with your wife.

To repair your marriage, you will have to confront your fear of conflict and learn how to express your needs clearly and openly. You may also need to learn to trust that other people are capable of hearing what you need and meeting those needs.

Perhaps you doubt your wife is capable of change, and you have given up on trying to get your needs met inside the marriage. You may need an infusion of hope and trust, combined with a commitment to being open with your wife about your needs or dissatisfaction. You may need help finding solutions.

The Intimacy Avoidance Affair:

If you answered YES to questions 1, 2, 5, 14, and 18, you fit this type.

You are afraid to get close to your wife. You find yourself fighting with her on a regular basis to avoid getting close to her and revealing your emotional vulnerability. You are also not emotionally invested in your AP and you can easily end the affair. Your affair served as a way to stay emotionally distant from your wife.

If you want to repair your marriage, you will need to learn how to develop an intimate relationship with your wife. This requires vulnerability and allowing yourself to be "seen" and loved as you are. You can work on this in therapy individually and/or with your wife.

The Affair Born Out of Unmet Emotional Needs:

If you answered NO to question 10 and YES to questions 4, 15, 17, and 22, you fit this type.

There is something in your marriage that makes you unhappy. You feel you need more than your wife is giving. You have even discussed your needs with your wife, and she has not made changes necessary to help fulfill your needs. You feel somewhat justified in having an affair because of this. However, you are not ready to give up on the marriage.

This is the most common reason that good men make the bad decision to have an affair. I encourage you to seek couples counseling after the initial turmoil has died down. You have an excellent chance of saving your marriage—if your wife stays and you learn how to express your needs to her in a way that helps her understand how important these issues are to you.

The Split Selves Affair:

If you answered NO to question 2 and YES to questions 3, 6, 15, and 17, you fit this type.

You feel devoted to your marriage and are trying to do everything right. You have made many sacrifices to make your marriage work, and now you feel the burden of subjugating your own needs for the needs of your family.

You are very involved with household activities and are probably known as an excellent parent and partner. However, you feel like the relationship has been unfair. Under this weight, you strayed from the marriage to get your needs met.

Most likely you feel loving toward your AP and may be having a tough time breaking ties with her. You want both a happy marriage and an AP because you now love both people.

This is another main reason couples find themselves in my office. There is an excellent chance you will have the marriage you want because you are capable of emotionally investing in a relationship.

The Entitlement Affair:

If you answered NO to questions 10 and 17 and YES to questions 5, 6, 11, and 12, you fit this type.

You feel like you deserve to have everything you want. You

have always been treated as special and you work hard to get what you believe you deserve. Few people have ever said no to you. Your parents gave you everything you wanted as a child. You feel little guilt about the affair you had.

Please take the Sexual Addiction Self-Assessment to see if this is part of your struggle. Please do NOT try to recover your marriage if you are only going to cheat again! Instead, get help from a therapist (individually) to work through your issues, whether it be with sexual addiction or with feeling like you should be able to have everything your way.

The Opportunistic/One Night Stand Affair:

If you answered YES to questions 7, 10, 16, 20, and 21, you fit this type.

These are unplanned, spontaneous affairs. Often people who have these types of affairs did not plan to do so. There is often no real issue in the marriage leading to the affair. In many cases, they involve a stranger. Generally, these are isolated incidents. Travels, such as business trips, alcohol, or drugs may contribute to the affair.

You probably feel a lot of guilt over this and fear being found out. Please take the Sexual Addiction survey to see if this is contributing to your struggle.

The Exit Strategy Affair:

If you answered NO to question 10 and YES to questions 5, 8, 13, and 19, you fit this type.

You are ready to end the marriage and are using an affair as a launching board to accomplish your goal. You may or may not have started the affair intentionally as a way to get out of your marriage, but you subconsciously hope she will find out you are cheating and dump you so you don't have to be the bad guy who divorced her. Ironically, you may prefer to be the bad guy who was caught cheating!

If you feel this way, it is time to meet with an individual therapist or minister to determine if this is true and, if so, how you can separate from your wife. At first, you may feel that you can win your wife back. It's true, you could win her back by following the strategies in this book... but you shouldn't even try because your heart isn't really in it.

Sexual Addiction Self-Assessment

Below is a Sexual Addiction Self-Assessment (Sex Addicts Anonymous
http://saa-recovery.org/IsSAAForYou/AreYouASexAddict/)
to help you determine if you have a problem with sexual addiction.

1. Do you keep secrets about your sexual behavior or romantic fantasies from those important to you? Do you lead a double life?
    Yes_____ No_____
2. Have your desires driven you to have sex in places or with people you would not normally choose?
    Yes_____ No_____
3. Do you need greater variety, increased frequency, or more extreme sexual activities to achieve the same level of excitement or relief?
    Yes_____ No_____
4. Does your use of pornography occupy large amounts of time and/or jeopardize your significant relationships or employment?
    Yes_____ No_____
5. Do your relationships become distorted with sexual preoccupation? Does each new relationship have the same destructive pattern which prompted you to leave the last one?
    Yes_____ No_____
6. Do you frequently want to get away from a partner after having sex? Do you feel remorse, shame, or guilt after a sexual encounter?
    Yes_____ No_____

7.   Have your sexual practices caused you legal problems? Could your sexual practices cause you legal problems?

    Yes_____ No_____

8.   Does your pursuit of sex or sexual fantasy conflict with your moral standards or interfere with your personal spiritual journey?

    Yes_____ No_____

9.   Do your sexual activities involve coercion, violence, or the threat of disease?

    Yes_____ No_____

10. Has your sexual behavior or pursuit of sexual relationships ever left you feeling hopeless, alienated from others, or suicidal?

    Yes_____ No_____

11. Does your preoccupation with sexual fantasies cause problems in any area of your life—even when you do not act out your fantasies?

    Yes_____ No_____

12. Do you compulsively avoid sexual activity due to fear of sex or intimacy? Does your sexual avoidance consume you mentally?

    Yes_____ No_____

If you answered "Yes" to more than one of these questions, we encourage you to seek help.

Material reprinted (with permission) from Sex Addicts Anonymous:

http://saa-recovery.org/

For more information about sexual addiction, please visit their website.

Works Cited or Used for Inspiration

Buehlman, K., Gottman, J. M., & Katz, L. (1992). How a couple views their past predicts their future-predicting divorce from an oral history interview. *Journal of Family Psychology, 5*(3-4), 295-318.

Post-traumatic Stress Disorder. (n.d.). Mayo Clinic: Diseases and symptoms. Retrieved from http://www.mayoclinic.org/diseases-conditions/post-traumatic-stress-disorder/basics/symptoms/con-20022540

Rider, K. V. (2011). Using a metaphor to help couples rebuild trust after an affair. *Journal of Family Psychotherapy, 22*(4), 344-348. doi: 10.1080/08975353.2011.627804

Snyder, D. K., Baucom, D. H., & Gordon, K. C. (2007). *Getting past the affair: A program to help you cope, heal, and move on—together or apart.* Guilford Press: New York.

Vaughan, P. (2003). *The monogamy myth: A personal handbook for recovering from affairs.* Third edition. William Morrow: New York.

Zemon Gass, G., & Nichols, W. C. (1988). Gaslighting: A marital syndrome. *Contemporary Family Therapy, 10*(1), 3-16.

Recommended Reading

How Can I Forgive You?: The Courage to Forgive, the Freedom Not To (Paperback – 2005) by Janis A. Spring

Transcending Post-infidelity Stress Disorder (PISD): The Six Stages of Healing (Paperback, 2009) by Dennis C. Ortman

Surviving an Affair (Hardcover, 2013) by Willard F. Jr. Harley and Jennifer Harley Chalmers

Divorce Busting: A Step-by-Step Approach to Making Your Marriage Loving Again (Paperback, 1993) by Michele Weiner-Davis

Not Just Friends: Rebuilding Trust and Recovering Your Sanity after Infidelity (Hardcover, 2010) by Shirley Glass

About the Author

Dr. Caroline Madden, MFT is a Los Angeles-based pro-marriage therapist and author of several relationship books. She specializes in helping marriage survive and thrive after an affair. For more information about her and her relationship coaching services, please visit her author website: www.CarolineMadden.com.

Thank You

I hope that you found *After a Good Man Cheats: How to Rebuild Trust & Intimacy With Your Wife* useful.

Please feel free to contact me with any feedback you may have: TherapyBurbank@gmail. I'd love to hear from you what in particular you found helpful and what you think should be included in future versions.

Would you like personal coaching? Contact me directly: TherapyBurbank@gmail.com or CarolineMadden.com.

All my best,

Dr. Caroline

More Books By Caroline Madden, MFT

How to Go From Soul Mates to Roommates in 10 Easy Steps

When Your Spouse Loses A Parent: What to Say & What to Do

Fool Me Once: Should I Take Back My Cheating Husband?

Blindsided By His Betrayal: Surviving the Shock of Your Husband's Infidelity

Would you like a FREE eBook?

As thanks for purchasing this book, my publisher would like to send you a free eBook. Visit their website to pre-order your free eBook:

http://trainofthoughtpress.com/get-a-book-for-free/